Mrs. MEYER'S

CLEAN HOME

No-nonsense advice that will inspire
you to **CLEAN** like the **DICKENS**

ILLUSTRATED and DESIGNED BY Werner Design Werks, Inc.

Mrs. MEYER'S CLEAN HOME

No-nonsense advice that will inspire you to **CLEAN** like the **DICKENS**

by *Mrs. Thelma A. Meyer*

 WELLNESS CENTRAL

 **MELCHER MEDIA**

NEW YORK   BOSTON

WELLNESS CENTRAL
HACHETTE BOOK GROUP
237 PARK AVENUE
NEW YORK, NY 10017

VISIT OUR WEB SITE AT www.HachetteBookGroup.com.

Wellness Central is an imprint of Grand Central Publishing. The Wellness Central name and logo are trademarks of Hachette Book Group, Inc.

PRODUCED BY **MELCHER MEDIA**   WWW.MELCHER.COM
124 West 13th Street, New York City, New York 10011

PRINTED IN CHINA   **FIRST EDITION: MARCH 2009**
10 9 8 7 6 5 4 3 2 1   LCCN: 2008933066   ISBN 978-0-446-54459-7

Mixed Sources
Product group from well-managed
forests and other controlled sources
www.fsc.org Cert no. DNV-COC-000054
© 1996 Forest Stewardship Council

To my family.
To all the mothers in the world who love and sacrifice for their families.
To God. (Cleanliness is next to godliness, after all!)

And to Vern Meyer, my husband of fifty-four years.
Without Vern, nothing would be possible, least of all this book.
He's made our house easy to clean, very comfortable, and spacious
by building, rewiring, refinishing, and enlarging it as we grew.
I can't imagine a better person with whom to build a home.

CONTENTS

INTRODUCTION

Meet Thelma   8

A Clean Outlook   10

Meet the Meyer Family   14

What to Clean When   20

Spring Cleaning   22

Fall Cleaning   24

Organizing Your Priorities   26

Use Good-for-You Cleaning Products   28

Your Cleaning Supply List   29

A Clean Day Every Day   32

CHAPTER 1 A CLEAN **KITCHEN**   34
How to tackle everything—including
the kitchen sink

CHAPTER 2 A CLEAN **BATHROOM**   62
Getting the shower, tub, and tiles sparkly clean

CHAPTER 3 A CLEAN **LIVING** ROOM   84
Cleaning the floors, the ceilings, the walls, and
the furniture—and of course the television too!

CHAPTER 4 A CLEAN **BEDROOM**   108
Beds and floors and even the baby's room

CONTENTS

CHAPTER 5 **A CLEAN HOME OFFICE**   128
Managing the room where you manage
your household

CHAPTER 6 **CLEAN LAUNDRY**   144
Keeping your colors bright and whitening
your whites. Plus removing those pesky stains

CHAPTER 7 **CLEAN NOOKS AND CRANNIES**   172
Your basements, attics, entryways, and all the
places in between

CHAPTER 8 **A CLEAN OUTDOORS**   190
Making outdoor space—from your garage
to your garden—a delightful place to be

AND!

Pets, Odors, and Pests   214

Glossary   224

About Mrs. Meyer's Clean Day   230

About the Contributors   232

Acknowledgments   233

Index   234

meet **THELMA**

Dear Friend,

Ever since my daughter Monica started Mrs. Meyer's Clean Day, back in 2001, people are always asking, "Is Mrs. Meyer a real person?" Well, I'm here to confirm it once and for all. My name is Thelma Meyer, and my daughter named her cleaning products after me to honor my good old-fashioned values. Nothing gives me more of a kick than when I introduce myself to someone who uses the products. Just recently I was waiting for a flight with a nice lady who was amazed when I told her who I was. What an honor!

I'm proud of the products that carry my name. The Mrs. Meyer's Clean Day products are powerful against dirt, grime, fingerprints, and the like. The philosophy is to make straightforward, honest cleaners that smell good and work like the dickens on dirt. They are also aromatherapeutic, which is a fancy word for healthy and good. But in my forty-plus years of cleaning house, I've learned that it's not just what you use to clean, it's how you clean, too.

Keeping up a house in a small town in Iowa while raising nine kids was no picnic, but I've discovered handy tricks for making day-to-day duties easier, monthly jobs seem like a cakewalk, and annual tasks a bit less grueling. That's where this book comes in.

So no, I'm not a cleaning superhero, but I really do exist. Grab your duster and follow me—we've got some work to do.

Wishing you a **CLEAN** and **HAPPY HOME,**

Mrs Thelma A. Meyer

a CLEAN OUTLOOK

My husband, Vern, and I got married in 1954. We lived in a trailer park in Des Moines with our twins until I got pregnant with our third child. "Thelma, it's time to get a house," Vern said. So we sold the forty-two-foot trailer and used the money from that as a down payment for a two-bedroom Cape Cod cottage-style house in Granger, Iowa. ⇒

We paid $12,000 for our new home, located about twenty miles northwest of Des Moines, in May of 1955. It was one of the first new houses in town.

And did we fill that house up! With nine kids, pets, kids' friends, and neighbors all around, I had to stay on top of things, but not drive myself too crazy. I adopted a "casually clean" policy. I believe in having a clean house, but I'm not one to have a perfect house. I like neatness and I like to see my home in an orderly fashion—I don't appreciate clothes or towels lying around—but I'm not a meticulous housekeeper either. Every day I'll do a little something, and when company comes, like my bridge friends, that's when I'll really get to work, making sure the windows are washed and all the fingerprints removed. But in general, the house just has to be clean enough and uncluttered. I like to focus on the big picture—getting the chores done daily so there's more time to enjoy life. It's all in the way you look at it. If you have a poor attitude, life is going to be a bear. You can look at your house and get overwhelmed and see all of the things that need tending to. Or you can tackle jobs little by little, whistling while you work, and know that even if your home doesn't shine from top to bottom, it's good enough for you.

I also believe that when you stay on top of things it's so much easier in the long run. Make a plan, and take the time to do chores right the first time. Don't stint once you commit to a task. That means throwing a little elbow grease into mopping up the bathroom floor and polishing the wood furniture. If you do it well, I promise you that there's pleasure to be had in that.

There's always going to be confusion when you're running a household, but there will be less of it when you take an organized approach. Figure out what works for you: Do you hate waking up to a not-too-tidy house? Take a few minutes before bed each night to do a little cleanup. Rather use that time for sleep? That's okay, too. I love freshly made beds, ship-shape surfaces and floors, and the smell of clean laundry. Some folks find ironing a soothing task. Do whatever suits your fancy.

In this book, you'll find tips for cleaning every room in the house and tending to the garden and patio, too. We'll go from kitchen to bathroom to office and every nook and cranny in between. I've shared the down-and-dirty tricks that I've been using for years! And since it never hurts to learn something new, I also asked friends and family to share their cleaning secrets with me. You'll find some great ideas in here—ketchup for cleaning copper and denture tablets for the toilet—that I just learned about, too. There are some sneaky ideas in here, including ways to get out those inevitable stains and foolproof solutions for dealing with life's little annoyances, from loosening a stuck drawer to getting bubblegum off a carpet. You'll also find that I have a lot of opinions on everything from clean curtains to parenting, in My House, My Rules.

My kids will weigh in with memories on what it was like to all live under one roof. (Boy, did it get crazy now and then.) Sometimes they remember things differently than I do, that's for sure. One thing they don't forget is how much they pitched in. Throughout this book, I mention how important it is to give your kids chores; it teaches them how to work hard and it will also make your life a little easier. My kids had to clean their rooms every Saturday, among other things. Be firm with your kids and tell it to them straight. Many parents just talk to their kids constantly—talk, talk, talk—but soon their kids will just stop listening. One of my favorite mottoes is SYE (save your energy). Don't ask young children if they want to clean their room. Just say, "Time to clean your room now." This avoids any possibility for disagreement.

I'm going to preach here what I practice: Use the least amount of water and energy possible. I was taught from an early age to save water. I was born in 1932, in the midst of the Great Depression, so water was hard to come by. My parents were Kansas farmers and hardly had anything to live on, and I remember my mom telling me that one winter we lived on nothing but tomato soup. We never had a lot, so we never consumed a lot. And that way of living was ingrained in me. Even today, I'll keep a bag in my purse and pick up litter as I see it. I'll reuse water too; I'll pour the water I use to wash my veggies into my houseplants. Waste not, want not. It's about respect for money and respect for our planet. Don't take what you don't need, and make do with what you have.

Also, care for yourself and your family by avoiding harsh disinfectants. The smell of a cleaning product shouldn't give you a headache. Read up on ingredients, making sure that anything you use is safe, especially if you have kids or pets around. You can get your house just as clean with a cleaning product that doesn't require gloves or masks. Check out my list of safe cleaning products on page 28. You'll see them cited throughout the book.

I like cleaning my house, I really do. And I want you to, as well. At the end of the day, try not to make yourself upset about housework. Why worry about it? You've just got to do what you can do and keep your home as neat as you can. It's all about enjoying yourself along the way and taking good care of your family, your community, and everything you love.

MEET the MEYER FAMILY

circa 1965

Thomas Henry

Timothy Joseph

1955

Vernis Henry Meyer
and
Thelma Anna (Renyer) Meyer
married August 25, 1954

1956

Monica Rose

4 Maria Joan

6 Jane Cecelia

8 Patrick John

1957

1960

1963

1958

1962

1965

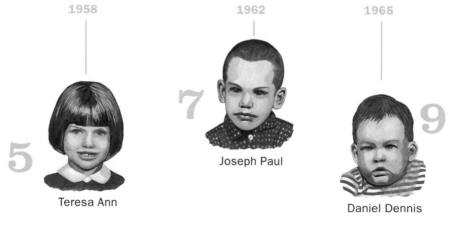

5 Teresa Ann

7 Joseph Paul

9 Daniel Dennis

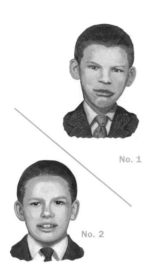

No. 1

No. 2

First we had the twins, Tom and Tim—and they were total opposites. **TOM** is the older twin; he was born before dinner and Tim was born after dinner. Tom's a diamond in the rough. He walked, striding across the floor, at ten months. He was a rebel and challenged us a lot, and he was always Mr. Busy. Whether it was cleaning pigpens or playing football, he just always had to be doing something. He works in sales and marketing, lives in Bend, Oregon, and has two children, Alison and Cale.

TIM was quieter and not as boisterous as Tom. He was always building things, losing tools in the yard while helping his dad fix cars, and generally tearing things apart to see what made them work. He spent his springs and summers mowing lawns, falls raking leaves, and winters shoveling snow. Now he's retired, after more than 20 years in the fiber-optics business. He lives in Las Vegas with his wife, Terry, and their dogs, Trouble and Twiggle. They're blessed with a daughter, Tammy, and son, Trevore.

Next up is **MONICA**—she was born six days before the twins turned one. She was the responsible one and could take charge, that Monica. She was like a little mother; she would take over for me if and when I needed it. As a youngster, she was the cook of the crew, but she also did outdoor jobs like walking beans, which meant cutting the weeds out of the beans with a corn knife. I remember a friend called for Monica one day and I said, "She's out walking beans." The friend later said to her, "I didn't know you had a dog named Beans." Monica is very fun, and she's a visionary too. She can just put her mind to something and bring it to fruition. She's the founder and CEO of Mrs. Meyer's Clean Day and Caldrea. She and her husband, David, live in Minneapolis and have two daughters, Aundrea and Calla.

No. 4

Thirteen months later came **MARIA**. As a child, she loved sports, being outside, and horses. But we couldn't afford to send her anywhere to ride horses, so she'd call up friends to see if she could ride with them. She has a wonderful sense of humor, and we always had fun teasing each other. She was very responsible and is to this day; as a family nurse practitioner in Des Moines, Iowa, she goes to meetings all over the United States, learning the latest information about keeping families healthy. Oh, and she loves to quilt; she and I could sit and quilt together all day. She and her husband, Pat, have three kids: Zach, Valerie, and Bart. Their first child, Bart, was killed in 2000 in a car accident.

No. 5

TERESA was born sixteen months later. She was rather quiet and loved to create, and was the smallest of the bunch—still is. And nowadays she's very serious and has a wonderful brain. She understands the mechanics of how things work really well. She's lived in Rochester, Minnesota, for most of her life and does fund-raising for a parochial school. She and her husband, Roger, have given us three grandkids: David, Lauren, and Claire.

No. 6

JANE arrived next, seventeen months later. She was a tomboy. She'd mow the lawn and help in the garden, and at six feet tall, she played basketball all through college. When she answers the phone you think it's me. She looks like me, has a lot of my mannerisms, and is kind of loud like me. She's very capable in the kitchen too. When she comes to visit, she'll say, "Mom, sit down!" and she takes over. She has a Ph.D. (which I jokingly tell her means "piled higher and deeper") in sports administration and lives in Iowa City, Iowa.

No. 7

Twenty-two months later came **JOE**. Now, Joe could just buffalo you. He was so smooth. I used to say he had a silver tongue because he was so slick. I remember going to school and telling his teacher, "Please don't let him buffalo you," because he could easily try and talk you out of something. And he's still like that now. He's very good-looking—with wavy black hair and blue eyes, he's just a gorgeous hunk of a man. He's an entrepreneur and lives with his wife, Susan, in Atlanta. They have two kids: Isabella and J. Paul.

No. 8

PAT came twenty months after Joe. Pat was quiet, a deep thinker, but the type you don't mess with. You might think someone like that, who's quiet and shy, would be a pushover, but he wasn't. He was persistent and a heck of a wrestler. And he's a very hard worker. He's worked for the Pella Corporation for many years and lives in Pella, Iowa, with his wife, Jackie, and their four children: Jacob, Madeline, John Ross (whom they call Jack), and Natalie.

No. 9

Last up is my baby, **DAN**. He was always reading and playing basketball. When Dan turned five, Vern said I could go back to work. So, after I put the kids to bed I would go to my job as a delivery-room nurse. When I'd come home in the morning, everyone would be at school except little Dan. I'd tell him, "You have to babysit Mom" so I could go rest. He'd answer the phone and the door. Dan loves children—he plays with his kids constantly. He's a pilot, so when he comes home from a trip his girls are all over his lap. They just think he's the cat's meow. He's my playful one. You get him started and he can keep the whole house roaring. He and his wife, Florence (we call her Flori), have Daniel, Dillon, Blayne, and Marin, and live in Billings, Montana.

they truly are my PRIDE and JOY

WHAT TO CLEAN WHEN

Keeping your house clean is largely about staying on top of what needs to be done when. Tending to your household regularly will save you time in the long run. The more time relaxing and the less time scrubbing, the better.

EVERY DAY	ONCE A WEEK	ONCE A MONTH
Wipe down the countertops	Wipe down appliances— inside and out	Clean the inside of the microwave
Wipe down the kitchen sink	Scrub the toilets, tubs, showers, and sinks	Scour the burner grates
Sweep the floors	Clean the mirrors	Clean the vent-hood filter
Take out the trash	Dust furniture, light fixtures, banisters, and shelves	Clean kitchen and bathroom cabinets
	Change bed linens	Wipe down the insides of medicine cabinets
	Do the laundry	Scrub grout
	Vacuum the carpets, drapes, and upholstery	Dust ceiling fans
	Mop the floors	Wipe down doorknobs and switch plates
		Clean electronics
		Vacuum moldings, baseboards, and heating and cooling vents
		Disinfect the garbage cans

ONCE EVERY **FEW MONTHS**	ONCE A **YEAR**
Clean the oven's interior	Clean the pantry (and toss expired items)
Clean the inside of the fridge	Air out the drapes
Thoroughly clean countertop appliances	Wash throw pillows
Vacuum the vents of the fridge, washer, and dryer	Sort through closets to decide what to keep, repair, donate, or recycle
Wash cotton slipcovers	
Wash comforters and duvet covers	
Wash bedroom pillows	
Vacuum and flip the mattresses	
Dust lamp shades	
Wash the windows	
Sweep the ceilings	
Clean the fireplace	

SPRING CLEANING

Go out and enjoy the warm weather—after you tend to these chores, of course.

GET CLEAR	Clean your windows inside and out with a solution of equal parts white vinegar and water. Use a squeegee in long strokes to dry them. Replace storm windows with screens. Polish window and door hardware.
LOOK AT WHAT'S UNDERFOOT	Vacuum the entire house, including baseboards, moldings, ceilings, and walls. Launder your area rugs and shampoo your carpets; you can rent a carpet cleaner from a hardware store or grocery store.
SHINE IT UP	Wax wood furniture and floors.
BE SAFE, NOT SORRY	Make sure the batteries in your smoke and carbon-monoxide detectors are working. Check your fire extinguishers to make sure they work, too.
BE FRIENDLY TO YOUR FURNITURE	Wipe down upholstery; steam-clean anything that's deeply soiled.

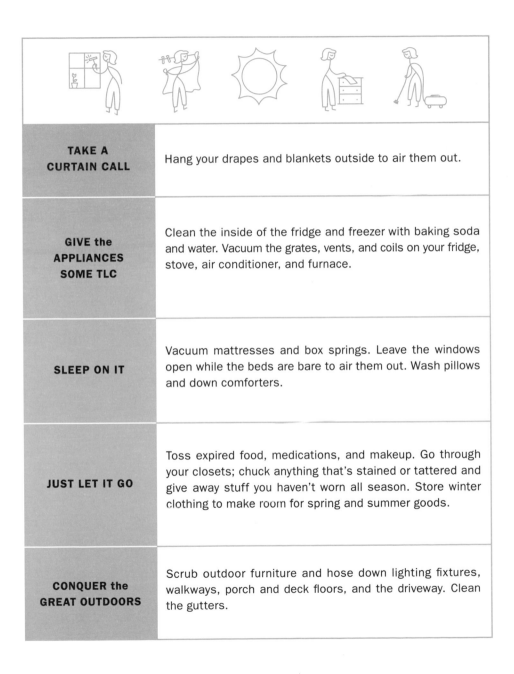

TAKE A CURTAIN CALL	Hang your drapes and blankets outside to air them out.
GIVE the APPLIANCES SOME TLC	Clean the inside of the fridge and freezer with baking soda and water. Vacuum the grates, vents, and coils on your fridge, stove, air conditioner, and furnace.
SLEEP ON IT	Vacuum mattresses and box springs. Leave the windows open while the beds are bare to air them out. Wash pillows and down comforters.
JUST LET IT GO	Toss expired food, medications, and makeup. Go through your closets; chuck anything that's stained or tattered and give away stuff you haven't worn all season. Store winter clothing to make room for spring and summer goods.
CONQUER the GREAT OUTDOORS	Scrub outdoor furniture and hose down lighting fixtures, walkways, porch and deck floors, and the driveway. Clean the gutters.

FALL CLEANING

Time to batten down the hatches! Don't let the cold weather catch you off guard.

MAKE YOUR WINDOWS SPARKLE	Clean the windows, paying extra attention to the ones on the south side of the house, to allow sunlight to stream in.
MINIMIZE LEAKS	Check the weather stripping around windows, doors, air conditioners, vents, and fans to make sure there are no gaps that will let heat escape and waste energy. Replace any weather stripping that looks old or worn. Consider placing plastic sheets over any particularly drafty windows.
BE SAFE	Change the batteries in smoke and carbon-monoxide detectors.
GET WARM and TOASTY	Clean your furnace filters of built-up dust and dirt by vacuuming. Or, if they're too far gone, buy brand-spanking-new ones.
CLEAN and INSPECT YOUR FIREPLACE	Vacuum the interior and screen, and check the flue. It's important to do this to make sure you don't have any dirt buildup before winter starts. Consider hiring a professional to do the work for you.

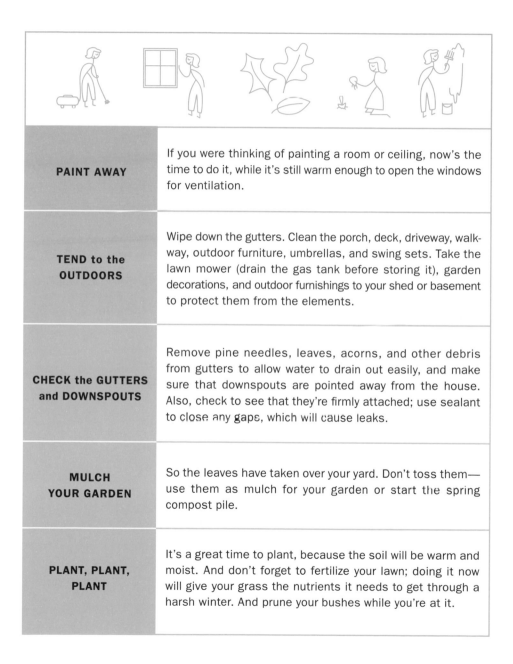

PAINT AWAY	If you were thinking of painting a room or ceiling, now's the time to do it, while it's still warm enough to open the windows for ventilation.
TEND to the OUTDOORS	Wipe down the gutters. Clean the porch, deck, driveway, walkway, outdoor furniture, umbrellas, and swing sets. Take the lawn mower (drain the gas tank before storing it), garden decorations, and outdoor furnishings to your shed or basement to protect them from the elements.
CHECK the GUTTERS and DOWNSPOUTS	Remove pine needles, leaves, acorns, and other debris from gutters to allow water to drain out easily, and make sure that downspouts are pointed away from the house. Also, check to see that they're firmly attached; use sealant to close any gaps, which will cause leaks.
MULCH YOUR GARDEN	So the leaves have taken over your yard. Don't toss them— use them as mulch for your garden or start the spring compost pile.
PLANT, PLANT, PLANT	It's a great time to plant, because the soil will be warm and moist. And don't forget to fertilize your lawn; doing it now will give your grass the nutrients it needs to get through a harsh winter. And prune your bushes while you're at it.

ORGANIZING YOUR

Life, like our homes, can get messy. If friends call to say they're heading over for an impromptu visit, but your house is a disaster—don't panic. Take a deep breath and do what we nurses call triage.

1 FOCUS on WHAT THEY'LL SEE FIRST

Shake out the welcome mat. Dust the entryway console. Sweep the floors, paying special attention to sofa and chair legs, where dust tends to gather.

2 ADD SHIMMER and SHINE

Quickly polish a silver vase, bowl, or candlestick, and place it in full view—perhaps on the coffee table or mantel. It'll make guests think everything looks as shiny and new as it does.

3 BEAUTIFY the BATHROOM

You know your guests are going in there at some point, so take a minute or two to wipe down the sink and counter, put out some colorful guest towels, straighten the bath mat, close the shower curtain, of course, and place a flower from the garden in a vase on the vanity. Turn off the lights and light a candle.

PRIORITIES

4 CLEAN UP the KITCHEN

This is the place where everyone tends to congregate. Make sure your sink is clear of dishes (put some in the oven if you have to), then wipe down the counters, stove top, and fridge. Put out a platter of fruit or cheese to distract them from any dirt.

5 COPE WITH SUSPICIOUS SMELLS

Change the cat litter, take out the garbage, or run the sink disposal. Make sure that anything with a rotten smell is cleared out and neutralized. You certainly don't ever want it to be said that your home has a less-than-appealing scent, that's for sure. In a pinch, make a pot of coffee; it will fill your house with a homey aroma. Plus, it's the hospitable thing to do!

6 DIM the LIGHTS and BREAK OUT the CANDLES

Dust bunnies all but disappear. And who doesn't look better by candlelight?

use GOOD-FOR-YOU CLEANING PRODUCTS

First, let's talk about chemicals. Not all of them are harmful—the air we breathe contains chemicals, after all—but many cleaning products and disinfectants contain chemicals that can pose health risks that we may not even know about yet. And they won't necessarily get your home any cleaner. It's not worth it! So my take is to use anything harsh sparingly, if at all, and instead opt for natural cleaning solutions. You'll find I suggest tried-and-true essentials throughout the book, like baking soda, lemon juice, and vinegar.

BAKING SODA

Also known as sodium bicarbonate, baking soda regulates pH balance, meaning it keeps things from being too acidic or too alkaline. So that's why baking soda is great for neutralizing (absorbing) smells in your fridge. It's mildly abrasive, too, so you can sprinkle it on most surfaces to clean them without worrying about scratching or leaving a residue.

LEMON JUICE

The acidic nature of lemon juice is ideal for dissolving anything from soap scum to hard-water deposits. You can mix it with olive oil for a natural furniture polish or sprinkle baking soda on half a lemon and use it to scrub your dishes.

VINEGAR

Vinegar is fermented wine, spirits, fruit, rice, grain, or honey. The key ingredient is acetic acid, which gives vinegar its sour taste, and also helps to kill a broad range of bacteria when used as a cleaning agent. Fill a spray bottle with equal parts water and distilled white vinegar and use it for anything from tackling appliances and sinks to shower stalls.

your CLEANING SUPPLY LIST

You needn't have all of these supplies stockpiled in your home, but they do come up throughout the book, so I thought a handy list would be a helpful thing. Having the right tools is always half the battle, but in a pinch, some all-purpose cleaning liquid, dishwashing liquid, detergent, cloths, baking soda, lemon juice, white vinegar, a good mop, and a solid broom will always do the trick. See page 224 for a glossary of selected terms.

GENERAL CLEANING, DUSTING, WIPING, and SCRUBBING

BRUSHES

Counter
Nylon-bristle
Soft-bristle
Stiff
Toilet
Toothbrush
Vegetable

BUCKETS, GLOVES, and MORE

Bucket or pail
Dustpan
Eyedropper
Rubber gloves
Spray bottle
Work gloves

CLEANING PRODUCTS

All-purpose cleaning liquid
Baby wipes
Baking soda
Borax
Carpet cleaner
Club soda
Cola
Countertop spray
Cream of tartar
Denture tablets
Dishwashing liquid
Distilled water
Hydrogen peroxide
Ketchup
Lemon juice
Oxygen bleach
Rubbing alcohol
Shampoo
Soap
Solvent cleaner
Surface spray
White vinegar
Window-cleaning liquid

CLOTHS, RAGS, SPONGES, and OTHER WIPERS

Big soft sponge
Brown paper
Chamois cloth
Cotton balls and swabs
Dry sponge
Dust cloth
Dusters
(extendable and feather)
Lint-free cloth
Microfiber cloth
Muslin cloth
Newspaper
Nylon scrubby pad
Old T-shirts, socks, and sheets
Paper towels
Polishing cloth
Scouring pads
Squeegee
Steel wool

MORE

your CLEANING SUPPLY LIST

SWEEPING, MOPPING, and VACUUMING

BROOMS	MOPS	VACUUMS
Angled	Dust	Handheld
Push	Floor	Stand-up
Hand	*(rag and sponge)*	Stick

STAIN REMOVAL and LAUNDRY

Clothesline

Delicate wash

Detergent *(baby and mild)*

Dry-cleaning solvent

Enzyme-based cleaner

Enzyme presoak

Fabric softener

Iron

Pretreatment product

Stain remover *(for carpeting, clothing, and upholstery)*

Talcum powder

Towel

Turkish towel

Upholstery shampoo

Zippered mesh bags

WAXING and POLISHING

Car wax

Furniture wax

Lemon juice

Linseed or jojoba oil

Olive oil

Paste wax

Polish (furniture and metal)

Vodka

your CLEANING SUPPLY LIST

ODOR FIXERS

Active charcoal
Chalk
Coffee grounds
Essential oil

Eucalyptus oil
Kitty litter
Lemon oil

for OUTDOORS

Hose
Mower
Watering can

plus, it's handy to have these around

Blow-dryer
Compressed air
Cornmeal
Dryer sheets
Lint roller
Paintbrush
Pipe cleaners
Plastic spatula
Poultice (stone)
Pumice stone
Putty knife

Rosemary
Safety glasses
Salt
Slice of white bread
Sodium bicarbonate
Straight pin
Tabasco sauce
Tinfoil
Toothpaste
Toothpick
Worcestershire sauce

a CLEAN DAY EVERY DAY

Chores can creep up on you and ruin a perfectly good Saturday if you're not careful. Traditionally, every day of the week was slated for a certain chore. Here's my list for what tasks to tackle each day. Even the best planners can have their schedules thrown into a tizzy, however. Blessed are the flexible, I always say. They shall never be bent out of shape!

MONDAY

LAUNDRY DAY

After Sunday's rest and relaxation (which for many of us means a lot of time outdoors), doing laundry is a good way to ease into the week. When you get home from work, do a few loads and feel good about having nice, clean clothes for the coming week.

TUESDAY

IRONING and MENDING DAY

Ironing, for many, is the most meditative of chores. As for mending, grab your pile of socks and shirts and get to work. If your clothes are beyond repair, cut them into rags to use for cleaning. Using paper towels is a waste of money and a bigger waste of paper. I also just discovered a great way to use the occasional orphaned sock: Slip it over your hand and wash windows with it!

WEDNESDAY

BEDROOMS and HOME OFFICE DAY

Changing the sheets is delightful, since sleeping on clean, fresh sheets is one of life's finest pleasures. Tackle your vacuuming and dusting, being sure to clean the windows too. No skimping under the bed!

THURSDAY

SHOPPiNG DAY

Grocery shopping on the weekends is not for the faint of heart—it's just too crowded for me. So grab your list and go on a Thursday evening instead, to enjoy a chaos-free store. Don't forget your coupons.

FRIDAY

LIVING ROOM DAY

Time to vacuum the sofa, carpet, and chairs, dust the electronics, and clean the glass on the television, which gets so dirty! Let the sunshine in by washing the windows, and wash the floors. Polish up your decorative bowls and frames—they're so nice to have out when company comes, or just to enjoy for yourself.

SATURDAY

BATHROOM and KITCHEN DAY

These rooms get oh-so-grimy—get up early, get them done, and do whatever you want with the rest of your weekend. Right after your morning coffee or tea, take on the kitchen: Attack the counters, sinks, and floors; wipe down the appliances; and polish up the faucets. Then make the bathrooms sparkle, washing the tiles and giving the tubs and toilets a good rubdown. Throw a little elbow grease into it and call it your weekend workout.

SUNDAY

REST and RELAX

Enjoy the fruits of all the week's work by spending time with the people you love or even with a good book and a nice piece of dark chocolate. That always does it for me.

CHAPTER 1

a clean KITCHEN

My kitchen is command central—it's where we all tend to gather, whether it's morning, noon, or night. And it gets busy. It was especially busy when the kids were young. Whether I was canning tomatoes, carrots, or beans, or the kids were coloring Easter eggs, baking chiffon cake, or doing their homework, there was always something going on. It was lived in, that's for sure. And that was just fine with me. ⟹

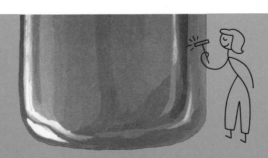

I never set out to have a spic-and-span kitchen; I'd rather have a lived-in one. So I don't clean just to be doing something—that's like watching paint dry. It's when I notice crumbs on the counter or dirt smears on the windows, then I take action. I'll tell you this: My husband never complained about my house-cleaning abilities. At least not to my face.

I taught my girls to clean as they cooked. To wipe up spills the second they happened. To rinse and soak pots and pans so they're almost clean before you even cleaned 'em. When they'd make a meal, there was hardly anything to do afterward. I also taught them about my very favorite secret cleaning weapons: baking soda, lemon, white vinegar, and dishwashing liquid. You can tackle just about the whole kitchen with these four items. And over the years, I've also learned that there are some things you can do to prevent messes in the first place: Use tinfoil to line your cookie sheets, muffin pans, and the oven, too. And brown your hamburger in a pan with extra-high sides to contain splatters so you won't have to wipe down your walls. It's all about knowing how to shave a few minutes off here and there, so you can enjoy your time in the kitchen cooking and laughing and sharing meals—not just cleaning and scrubbing.

the KITCHEN SINK 39

washing the SINK 39
flushing the DRAIN 39
cleaning the FAUCETS 39
getting SINKS SQUEAKY-CLEAN 40

the COUNTERTOP APPLIANCES 41

mastering the MIXER 41
caring for the COFFEEMAKER 41
battling the BLENDER 41
giving the TOASTER SOME TLC 41
cleaning the ELECTRIC CAN OPENER 41

the WALLS and WINDOWS 42

being RUTHLESS on BACKSPLASHES 42
getting GREASE STAINS off the WALLS 42
whipping WINDOWS into SHAPE 42

the OVEN, POTS, and SILVERWARE 43

cleaning the VENT HOOD 43
scrubbing a VERY MESSY STOVE TOP 43
scouring the INTERIOR 43
cleaning the KNOBS 43
washing a BURNED POT 43
making SAUCEPANS SHINE and GRIDDLES GLEAM 44
getting SILVERWARE SPOTLESS 46
being SHARP about KNIVES 47

the **MICROWAVE** 48

the **DISHWASHER** 49

the **REFRIGERATOR** 50
wiping down the FRIDGE 50
cleaning the COILS 50
DEFROSTING the FREEZER 50

as for the **SMELLY STUFF** 51
giving that GRIMY GARBAGE CAN a GOOD CLEAN 51
why does my SINK STINK? 51

the **TABLE** 52
the TOP 52
perfecting PLACE MATS 52

the **CABINETS** 52
tackling the INTERIORS 52
checking on the PRODUCE 52
cracking down on CABINETS 53
conquering the COUNTERTOPS and CUTTING BOARDS 54

cleaning the **KITCHEN FLOORS** 57

getting canny about **CANNING** 58

TOOLBOX

BRUSHES
Nylon-bristle
Toothbrush

BUCKETS, GLOVES, and MORE
Bucket or pail
Rubber gloves
Spray bottle

CLEANING PRODUCTS
All-purpose
cleaning liquid
Baking soda
Borax
Club soda
Cream of tartar
Dishwashing liquid
Flour
Ketchup
Lemon juice
Rubbing alcohol
Salt
Tabasco sauce
Toothpaste
White vinegar
Worcestershire sauce

CLOTHS, RAGS, SPONGES, and OTHER WIPERS
Cotton swab or toothpick
Newspaper
Nylon scrubby pad
Paper towels
Rag
Scouring pad
Soft cloth
Sponge
Steel wool

SWEEPING, MOPPING, and VACUUMING
Broom
Mop
Vacuum
with attachments

WAXING and POLISHING
Furniture polish
Linseed or jojoba oil

ODOR FIXERS
Active charcoal
Coffee grounds
Kitty litter
Lemon juice

HANDY to HAVE THESE AROUND
Plastic spatula
Poultice
Rosemary

the KITCHEN SINK

Washing the Sink

Hot soapy water and a sponge should get most sinks clean, but a little dishwashing liquid can really make it shine. If you have a spot you need to wipe out, go to the guide on page 40.

Flushing the Drain

With the amount of food I cook in my kitchen, it's no wonder the drain gets clogged as often as it does. I'm not a fan of heavy chemicals like bleach (that smell!), so to clear clogs right up use this homemade recipe: Pour half a cup of baking soda down the drain, then half a cup of distilled white vinegar; cover the drain with a wet rag. After five minutes or so, pour some boiling water down. No more clogs. Or you can add half a cup of salt to the drain, followed by boiling water. And whatever you do, never, ever pour grease down the drain. Instead, take a tin can out of the recycling and pour your grease in that. Once it hardens, you can throw the whole thing out. It's an old standby that will save you money, time, and a plumber's visit.

Cleaning the Faucets

Whether your faucets are chrome, stainless steel, copper, brass, or nickel, all you need to do is apply dishwashing liquid and warm water, then buff, buff, buff with a good cloth to make them shine bright. Keep a toothbrush handy and use it to clean the base and the crevices where the faucet meets the sink. If lime and mineral deposits are plaguing your faucets, try wrapping them in a white-vinegar-soaked paper towel for an hour. After you remove the wet paper towel, buff those faucets with a dry paper towel. That should get them shiny again.

my HOUSE, my RULES

You need to make work **FUN** for kids so that they're inspired to **GET THINGS DONE.** Every Saturday morning, I'd put a list of **CHORES** on the refrigerator door. Whoever got up first got to pick the job he or she wanted to do. And the last guy had to take what was left. They all had to **SIGN THEIR NAMES** next to the chores they picked so I knew who was responsible for each task.

GETTING SINKS SQUEAKY-CLEAN

Let me let you in on a little secret. If someone—say, your mother-in-law—is heading over for a visit, cleaning your sink should be one of the things on your list. A sparkly sink forgives a host of other sins (like forgetting her birthday year after year).

COPPER	Ketchup isn't just for hamburger. Here's a fun home remedy I just learned about: Squirt some into your copper sink, rub it in with a soft rag, and rinse with cold water. Works like magic! Or a little hot, soapy water will do a fine job, too.
PORCELAIN and ACRYLIC	Rust stains on porcelain and acrylic can be a pickle. Here's what you do: Mix together two parts all-purpose cleaning liquid to one part lemon juice to get that wretched spot out quick. I also don't like the brown cast I sometimes get in my white porcelain sink. So if it's not white enough after scouring with a powder, rub it with a cloth soaked in borax. And when the sink starts looking scuffed up, fill it with hot water, add a few sprigs of rosemary, and let it all sit overnight.
SOLID SURFACE	These sinks clean up in a snap; just use a soft cloth, and wipe in a circular motion with a mixture of equal parts white vinegar and warm water. Easy as pie.
STAINLESS STEEL	Soak a rag in all-purpose cleaning liquid and warm water and rub with the grain to avoid scratches—and stay away from abrasive cleaners at all costs. Make sure to dry the sink thoroughly or else water marks will form, and who needs those?
STONE	Avoid using lemon juice and vinegar on granite, marble, or limestone; you may damage the finish. Instead, just use warm water and dishwashing liquid.

the COUNTERTOP APPLIANCES

Mastering the Mixer

My standing mixer was always a mess (hey, yours would be, too, if you baked as many birthday cakes as I did). There were times when I'd clean it right after using it, then take it out and think, This doesn't look clean at all! So now I'm even more careful. Follow these guidelines: Soak the beaters in hot, sudsy water to get any residue off before hand-washing them (only stainless-steel ones can be placed in the dishwasher). Put the bowl in the dishwasher and then tackle the base: Wipe the sides down with warm water before the drips and splashes harden. Then use a cotton swab or a toothpick to get into all those nooks and crannies, where batter tends to stick—don't forget the vent. When the base is dry, wrap the cord around it and away it goes.

Caring for the Coffeemaker

Over the years, I've learned a few tricks for keeping this appliance perking along. Every time you use it, clean the carafe with warm, soapy water so that oils won't build up and ruin the taste of your brew. When the coffeemaker seems to be getting slow, pour equal parts white vinegar or lemon juice and water into the reservoir. Run a cycle, then run two more cycles with hot water to flush it out.

Battling the Blender

Soak the blade and other removable parts in warm, sudsy water, and wipe down the base (don't submerge this part!) with dishwashing liquid. The glass jar can be placed in the dishwasher. Once every dozen or so times you use it, treat your blender to a bath. Fill the jar halfway with warm water and a few squirts of dishwashing liquid, then put it on the base and blend on low speed for thirty seconds.

Giving the Toaster Some TLC

Clean out your toaster regularly or else those crumbs will cause a burnt odor—or worse yet, catch on fire! Line the tray with foil, and replace the foil every week. After every, say, twenty or so uses (with my family that meant practically every day, for Pete's sake), unplug the toaster, let it cool, and wipe down the interior with a damp cloth. Afterward, soak the racks in warm water with a squirt of dishwashing liquid.

Cleaning the Electric Can Opener

Soak any removable parts in warm water and dishwashing liquid. Dip a toothbrush in baking soda and water and use it to get at any tough food residue, then dry the appliance thoroughly to make sure it doesn't rust.

the WALLS and WINDOWS

Being Ruthless on Backsplashes

When spaghetti sauce splatters, wipe it up with warm, sudsy water. It's so much easier to do right away, before stains have time to set.

Getting Grease Stains off the Walls

There's no way around grease getting on your kitchen walls, so your best bet is to paint your kitchen using gloss or semigloss paint. With grease, time is of the essence. Get at those stray grease spots immediately with a clean rag, hot water, and a little dishwashing liquid.

Whipping Windows into Shape

Your kitchen windows can get really mucked up with all the grease from cooking. I never use commercial cleaning products on my windows—because my homemade wash works wonders (if I do say so myself). Just mix together one quart of water, one tablespoon of dish-washing liquid, two teaspoons of white vinegar, and a generous splash of rubbing alcohol. (Don't worry too much about measuring; just use your common sense.) Apply the solution with crumpled-up pieces of newspaper—the rough finish absorbs the mixture well and just really wipes the windows clean. I keep all my cleaning recipes up on my kitchen door—they've been there so long they're getting brown. But I'll never take them down.

WASTE NOT WANT NOT

I'm the first to admit I'm frugal, let me tell you: Sometimes I'll even make my own rags! (I prefer them to sponges—you can use them for everything.) One day my sister-in-law Cleta Renyer (Think I had it rough with nine kids? She raised thirteen on a dairy farm in Kansas!) was helping me clean up after dinner, saw a bunch of my homemade rags, and said, "Thelma, I cannot believe you did this!" But I did, and this is how: You know how your washcloths get thin in the middle? Cut them in half, put the thin centers to the outside and the good, thick parts in the middle, then stitch them back together. Now you've got nice, heavy rags for cleaning, and they don't take long to make at all! Always wash them out right away so they don't sit with dirt in them, because otherwise they'll get really ugly.

the OVEN, POTS, and SILVERWARE

Cleaning the Vent Hood

This little chore has to be done at least two or three times a year, and more often if you cook a lot. When it's about that time, just take off the metal filter, soak it in the sink in hot, soapy water, and then put it in the dishwasher. The grease will come right off—with minimal effort on your part. Wipe the exterior of the hood with hot, sudsy water.

Scrubbing a Very Messy Stove Top

Our stove top always took a beating in the summertime, because that was canning time. And nothing—not even nine children—can make the level of mess that canning can. Whether your stove top is glass-ceramic, porcelain, or stainless steel, the best thing to do is wipe up spills immediately with a damp cloth so stains won't harden. If you do have a tough stain, soften it up with hot water for a minute or two, sprinkle some baking soda on it, and wipe it clean with a rag. Take off those metal burner grates and put them in the sink to soak in soapy water. Meanwhile, wet rags in warm water and let them sit on the stove top for a while to loosen the gunk before wiping it clean with baking soda and warm water.

Scouring the Interior

Canning doesn't get the oven that dirty—but baking does, and the girls and I did a lot of it. I hate cleaning the oven, but it has to be done. (And I've never had an oven that truly cleans itself.) You won't need to contend with smelly fumes from chemical cleaners if you do as I do: Pour salt onto any fresh stains; it will absorb the food and allow the mess to be easily wiped clean. For general cleaning, sprinkle the interior with baking soda, spritz it with water, and let it sit overnight. Take out the racks and scrub them with steel wool to get off any grime. And then make sure to line the oven and broiler with foil—it will make cleanup even easier the next time.

Cleaning the Knobs

Those knobs can get so greasy from cooking and baking! If they're plastic and come off easily, run them through the dishwasher on the gentle cycle. If you can't remove them, sponge them off with warm water and dishwashing liquid.

WASHING A BURNED POT

When the kids or I would leave a pot on the stove too long (it didn't happen often, but it happened), we'd create a home remedy. Here's what you do: Fill the pot with equal parts water and white vinegar, add some salt, heat the mixture over a medium flame until the vinegar boils, and then remove the pot from the heat and let it soak overnight.

MAKING SAUCEPANS SHINE and GRIDDLES GLEAM

Nice pots and pans make a real difference, so my advice? Get good ones and take good care of them.

ALUMINUM It's better to hand-wash aluminum cookware in warm, soapy water than to stick it in the dishwasher, because the ultra-hot water and minerals in some dishwashing detergents can cause mineral-deposit stains over time. If you do get a stain, fill the pot with two to three tablespoons of cream of tartar and a quart of water; boil the mixture for five to ten minutes, then clean with a scouring pad and dishwashing liquid.

CAST IRON Cast-iron pots are heavy and retain heat like a charm. Some come pre-seasoned (or coated with cooking oil to provide a nonstick surface). If yours didn't come preseasoned, you can coat the interior with cooking oil and place it in a 350-degree oven for an hour; take it out and dry it with paper towels. To clean cast iron, wipe it out immediately with hot water (no soap needed, and don't submerge it) and some olive oil to flavor it. If necessary, you can use a nylon scrubby pad, but don't use anything too abrasive, and don't put the pan in the dishwasher. If it starts to get sticky over time, then scrub the surface with steel wool before reseasoning it.

CERAMIC and GLASS-CERAMIC These pots and pans are quick to heat up and quick to cool down—and quite beautiful too. To clean them, combine equal parts salt and flour with a little white vinegar. Apply this to the inside and outside of the pan and let sit for ten minutes before rinsing in hot water and drying thoroughly.

COPPER Don't put copper pans in the dishwasher. As you would with ceramic, combine equal parts salt and flour with a little white vinegar. Let the mix sit on the inside and outside of the pan for ten minutes, then rinse in hot water and dry thoroughly. If the surface is tarnished, try squeezing some ketchup onto it; after a few minutes, wipe it up.

**ENAMELED
CAST IRON**

Sturdy and able to retain heat well, enameled cast iron doesn't need to be seasoned and can be washed in hot, sudsy water with a nylon scrubby pad. Never use steel wool or scouring powder. You can put these dishes in the dishwasher, unless they have plastic handles.

GLASS

Let glass cookware cool completely before submerging it in water, and never move it directly from the fridge to the hot oven—it may crack. It can also crack if cleaned with abrasive cleansers or steel wool. Just use a sponge and hot, soapy water. To remove burned-on matter from starchy or sugary goods, soak in hot water and baking soda, then scour with more baking soda; its slightly abrasive texture will remove the grime. Sometimes the glass cookware that you use on the stove top gets dark mineral spots on it: Wipe them out by filling the pot with white vinegar; let it boil for fifteen minutes, then clean as usual.

NONSTICK

Wash with a soft sponge or nylon scrubby pad and hot, soapy water (abrasive cleansers and steel wool will scratch the surface). Make sure to remove all residue or else it'll harden over time and cause a sticky mess. If your pan is discolored, that means there's residue on it; fill it with water and two squirts of dishwashing liquid. Let the solution simmer to loosen any grime. When stacking nonstick pans, place a paper towel in between each piece to avoid scratches. And use plastic utensils!

SILICONE

Made of synthetic rubber, silicone is naturally nonstick and a snap to clean. Just wash in hot, soapy water or toss in the dishwasher.

**STAINLESS
STEEL**

Wash in warm, soapy water and dry immediately so you don't get water stains. Either use a soft sponge or one specifically made for stainless steel to avoid scratching the surface.

GETTING **SILVERWARE** SPOTLESS

Before you polish your silverware to a high shine, make sure to rinse it in warm water and mild detergent to get any dust off, and thoroughly dry each piece. Here's how to get a handle on everything from stainless steel to silver.

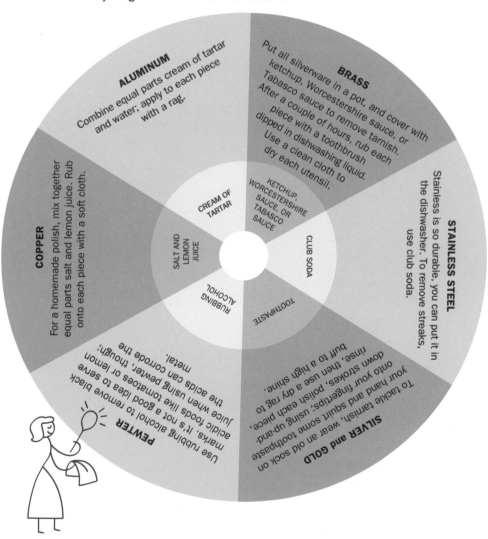

ALUMINUM
Combine equal parts cream of tartar and water; apply to each piece with a rag.

BRASS
Put all silverware in a pot, and cover with ketchup, Worcestershire sauce, or Tabasco sauce to remove tarnish. After a couple of hours, rub each piece with a toothbrush dipped in dishwashing liquid. Use a clean cloth to dry each utensil.

STAINLESS STEEL
Stainless is so durable, you can put it in the dishwasher. To remove streaks, use club soda.

SILVER and GOLD
To tackle tarnish, wear an old sock on your hand and squirt some toothpaste onto your fingertips; using up-and-down strokes, polish each piece. Rinse, then use a dry rag to buff to a high shine.

PEWTER
Use rubbing alcohol to remove black marks. It's not a good idea to serve acidic foods like tomatoes or lemon juice when using pewter, though; the acids can corrode the metal.

COPPER
For a homemade polish, mix together equal parts salt and lemon juice. Rub onto each piece with a soft cloth.

CREAM OF TARTAR

KETCHUP, WORCESTERSHIRE SAUCE, OR TABASCO SAUCE

SALT AND LEMON JUICE

CLUB SODA

RUBBING ALCOHOL

TOOTHPASTE

BEING SHARP ABOUT KNIVES

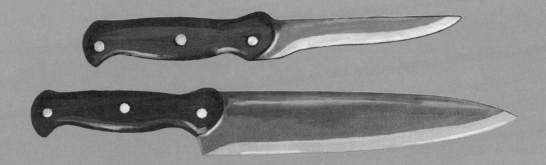

If someone has been nice enough to give you a set of good knives, you know how they can make SLICING and DICING as easy as pie. They'll last you a lifetime if you take care of them. Food residue will damage the blades, so make them last by cleaning them immediately after every use. Don't wash them in your dishwasher since the HIGH TEMPERATURES are HARMFUL. Mild soap and water will do the trick. Dry them off right away and store them in a WOODEN BLOCK rather than a silverware drawer. It will prevent hands from accidentally grabbing at SHARP blades.

the MICROWAVE

I fought buying a microwave for a long time. I didn't think I needed one, because I had a trusty steamer that kept food warm. But when the kids started coming home at different times—from sports or piano practice—we just went ahead and bought one. Clean it like this: Put a wet rag inside and turn the microwave on for a minute; the steam will melt those pesky grease spots so you can wipe them down really quickly. Use dishwashing liquid to clean the exterior and the control panel. And cover food with wax paper or paper towels to keep stuff from splattering all over. To tackle odors, mix half a cup of lemon juice and a cup of water and heat the solution on high for two minutes, leaving the door open afterward for an hour or so to air the microwave out.

WASTE NOT WANT NOT

When I'm not sure what to make for dinner, all I have to do is rifle through the fridge to check out the leftovers (most things can last for five days). I mix those leftovers all together in one big pot to create a new meal. I call this dinner Muskoe, because everything must go! Sometimes I combine mashed potatoes with vegetables and gravy; other times it's meat with tomato sauce, beans, and rice. Most things can go together, and taste pretty good to boot.

ah, the MEMORIES

"My mom was a **TOUGH COOKIE**—you learned pretty quick not to mess with her. And as the last of nine, I felt it was easier to **COMPLY** than to try to match wits or get out of doing what she said. But my sister **MARIA** didn't always feel the same way. Around the holidays, there were A LOT OF POTS AND PANS that needed to be cleaned. And we had a **SMALL DISHWASHER** that couldn't fit everything, so you had to wash them by hand. Almost every time there was a big meal and we had to do the dishes, Maria would announce, 'I have to go to the **BATHROOM**.' And she would never come back. We called it 'DISHPAN DIARRHEA.'"

— Dan (No. 9)

the DISHWASHER

I've worn out a bunch of dishwashers in my day. The kids would put plates in there without rinsing them first, and little pieces of bone and peelings would clog the washer up. So now I'm more careful when loading and cleaning mine. About once a week, wipe down the outside of the door—whether it's plastic or stainless steel—with warm water and dishwashing liquid. Every once in a while, grab an old toothbrush, pull out the racks, and scrub them with warm water, including the wheels, which tend to get really dirty. Frequently check the drain and reservoir for food scraps. If you're seeing smudge marks on your plates and residue at the bottom of your glasses, fill the detergent cup with white vinegar. Run a cycle with the dishwasher empty, then sprinkle borax around and leave it there overnight to soak. In the morning, wipe the inside down and it'll be good as new. Then, in between uses, toss some baking soda on the floor of the machine and you'll never have dishwasher odors again.

WASTE NOT WANT NOT Why throw out zip-top plastic bags just because there are a few cracker crumbs in them? I never do. Wash them, air-dry them, and use them over and over. No reason not to.

my HOUSE, my RULES

Never, ever bring your kids to the **GROCERY STORE!** That's just asking for trouble. Until, that is, they're old enough that you can put them to work **GETTING THE DEALS.** I'd rip coupons out of the newspaper, and because there were limits—you could buy only one gallon of milk or a dozen oranges or whatever— I'd go to the neighbors and ask if I could have their **COUPONS** if they weren't using them. Then I'd line the kids up at the checkout counters, each holding the same coupons. We'd do this at two or three stores.

the **REFRIGERATOR**

Wiping Down the Fridge

My nose lets me know when it's time to clean the fridge. Whenever I smell the beginning of an odor, I'll find something back in there that has started to mold and I'll know it's time for a cleaning. The exception to this rule, of course, back when I had kids at home, was when one of them spilled juice or broke an egg— then I'd have to deal with it right away. So when your nose lets you know, unplug the fridge, take everything out, and wipe the inside and all the shelves with warm water and dishwashing liquid. Soak any removable racks or drawers in the sink with warm, sudsy water. You can place a box of baking soda inside to absorb odors (replace it every three months or so), or even fill a tray with coffee grounds, unscented kitty litter, or active charcoal (the kind you'd get for an aquarium) for the same effect.

Cleaning the Coils

Twice a year, use your vacuum's brush attachment to clean those dusty coils— they're probably on the back of your fridge. This is important, because when dirt builds up the appliance runs less efficiently. And clean underneath the fridge while you're at it.

Defrosting the Freezer

Don't forget to clean the freezer every so often—I know it's a pain, but you just have to do it. Especially old freezers, because they get full of frost. You'll have to turn the appliance off and take everything out. Place stuff in a cooler or even the sink. And here's a tried-and-true trick: Put a pan of boiling water inside the freezer to melt all the frost. Of course, you have to make sure you have something to catch the drips—a garbage bin works well. Use a plastic spatula (metal scratches!) to scrape excess ice from the walls and

WASTE NOT WANT NOT

Over the years, I've learned to get the most out of my condiments. I add a tiny bit of water to my ketchup bottle when it's getting down to the bottom, shake it up good, and get five to ten more uses out of it.

racts. Then use a rag dampened with hot water and baking soda to fight odors and clean those racks, shelves, walls, and corners. (Don't use soap here, because the fragrance can be absorbed by your food, and who needs that?) Dry the interior with a cloth, turn the appliance back on, and wait until it cools all the way down again (about thirty minutes) before putting your food back in. To keep it cleaner in the future, wipe drips off your ice-cream containers and such before stowing them.

AS FOR the
SMELLY STUFF

Giving That Grimy Garbage Can a Good Clean

This is never fun—but you just have to do it. I keep my garbage cans under the sink, and I make sure they're always lined with plastic grocery bags and that they get emptied pretty frequently. I never had the smell of garbage in my kitchen, because I'd insist that the kids took it out. Air out your pails occasionally by bringing them outside, and whenever they get grungy, wipe them down with warm water and baking soda and use a nylon-bristle brush to get off any nasty stuff. Then sprinkle some borax on the bottom to keep mold and bacteria from growing.

Why Does My Sink Stink?

If there's a lingering smell and you're just not sure where it's coming from, check the garbage disposal. Toss a few lemon or orange peels down there and grind them up for a nice, fresh scent.

my HOUSE, my RULES

I had a **DINNER BELL** that I'd ring when it was time to eat. We lived near a park, and oftentimes the boys would be **PLAYING** there from morning until early evening. Well, all I had to do was **RING THIS BELL**, and not only would they hear it from **MILES** away, but all the neighbors did, too.

the TABLE

The Top

Wipe up spills immediately so that you don't get water marks; use place mats and coasters to protect the surface. Wipe the top with a cloth dampened with dishwashing liquid and water. (Instructions for cleaning different kinds of kitchen tables are the same as those for furnishings in the living room; see page 102.)

Perfecting Place Mats

Cotton place mats with no stains can be washed in a regular cycle with T-shirts and so forth. Wash those with oil stains (butter, olive oil) in hot water, which will help melt the stains; if stains remain, don't dry the place mats (the dryer will set the stains); rewash and air-dry them. Plastic place mats should be wiped down with warm water and dishwashing liquid.

WASTE NOT WANT NOT

If the kids didn't want to eat their entire dinner, I'd put their plates right in the fridge. And if they came running in an hour later saying "Mom, I want a cookie!" oh, no, they'd have to eat their dinner first—straight from the fridge. They soon learned to eat it when it was hot, let me tell you.

the CABINETS

Tackling the Interiors

About once a year, take everything out of the pantry and use your vacuum's handheld attachment to suck up crumbs—you know you have 'em. Then wipe those shelves down with warm water and dishwashing liquid. Before you put everything back, take inventory. My cabinets are always jam-packed with boxes of pasta, jars of jelly, and cans of veggies. And those goods don't last forever, so every now and then I'll look around in there and toss what's expired. Keep these numbers in mind: Unopened salad dressing, pasta, and rice last about a year, cooking oil about six months, and canned food about two years. But it's tough to play the guessing game, so write the month that you buy everything right on the packaging. It makes the purging process a lot easier. And it's important to label certain things too. My mother-in-law, Clara Meyer, always came to help out when I had a new baby. One day she stopped by and made us all corn bread, but she used salt instead of sugar! She had thick glasses, you see, so it was hard to tell one from the other.

Checking on the Produce

Keep an eye and nose on those potato and onion bins. Rifle through the bunch now and then to see if anything's gone bad, as one rotten potato or onion will spoil the whole lot.

CRACKING DOWN on CABINETS

No kids were ever allowed in my pantry. And I'll give you one good reason why: raisins up the nose. When Dan was three, he ran up to me sniffling like you wouldn't believe. "Do you have a cold?" I asked. Before he could answer, I saw something black sticking out of his left nostril. Turned out he had raisins stuck up there. I grabbed my tweezers and pulled them all out, or so I thought. "There's more!" he said. And then I pulled out two more. He had stuffed them so high I wasn't sure how he breathed. But I digress! Little hands means smudgy cabinets, so here are your best ways to clean them.

WOOD	My cabinets are birch—a very dense wood. You can't do much damage to it, and it cleans up in a snap. For any type of wood cabinet, though, just wipe down the doors with mild dishwashing soap and water—going with the grain—whenever they look like they need it, and dry them immediately with a soft cloth so they don't warp. And here's a nifty trick: Put furniture polish on the doors after cleaning them. It will keep them from getting so soiled in the future.
LAMINATE	These cabinets scratch like you wouldn't believe, so avoid rough sponges and abrasive cleaners; instead, wipe them with dishwashing liquid and a bit of warm water—if you use too much, it can get into the seams and cause the cabinets to warp. They tend to stain, too; draw stains out by applying a baking-soda-and-water paste, then carefully lifting the paste with a soft cloth.
STAINLESS STEEL	Stainless cabinets (especially those with a glossy finish) tend to show annoying fingerprints. To get rid of the marks quickly, dampen a soft cloth with dishwashing liquid and warm water and clean with the grain, then dry immediately with a separate cloth to avoid water marks. Stainless is prone to scratches too, but you can remove minor ones by buffing the surface with a nylon pad (again, going with the grain so you don't scratch it even more).
THERMOFOIL	This kind of cabinet is made of medium-density fiberboard topped with vinyl. It's really easy to care for—just clean it like you would laminate.

CONQUERING the COUNTERTOPS and CUTTING BOARDS

Getting your counters to sparkle usually just requires a little hot, soapy water and some elbow grease. Here are some other things to consider.

MATERIAL	METHOD
ACRYLIC	Just dishwashing liquid and warm water will do the trick.
CERAMIC TILE	Dilute one capful of rubbing alcohol in a gallon of water, and use a toothbrush to get into those grout lines.
LAMINATE	You can use a mixture of equal parts white vinegar and water, or simply fill a spray bottle with club soda and give the surface a spritz as needed.
LINOLEUM	When Vern and I moved into our Granger house (more than fifty years ago!), we had pink linoleum counters. Pink—can you believe that? Linoleum tends to stain, so right when something spills, sprinkle some baking soda on the mess and wipe it up with warm water.
GRANITE	Never use lemon juice, vinegar, or anything else acidic to clean granite; you'll get deep scratches. For that matter, try not to spill anything on granite, either—it stains very easily. If you do get a stain, you can apply a solution called a poultice (buy it at the hardware store) to literally suck the stain out. In general, clean granite with dishwashing liquid and warm water, and blot it dry to keep water spots at bay.

MATERIAL	METHOD
SOLID SURFACE	I use baking soda on my Formica solid-surface (high-density acrylic) counters. It's mildly abrasive (rub gently), but it doesn't leave a telltale mark on your finish.
STAINLESS STEEL	Clean it with dishwashing liquid, using a soft cloth and rubbing with the grain to minimize scratches, or simply use a damp microfiber cloth—it'll pick up dirt really easily, no cleaning products needed.
BUTCHER BLOCK	Use dishwashing liquid and just a bit of warm water—too much may warp the surface. Wood counters tend to hold bacteria, so about once a month, wipe the surface with white vinegar to kill the bacteria fast. For a quick homemade polish, mix up equal parts lemon juice and olive oil.
CUTTING BOARDS	After chopping, dicing, or what have you, it's important to sanitize cutting boards right away with hot, soapy water to kill any bacteria. It's not a bad idea to use one board for veggies and another for meat, so as not to cross-contaminate either one. For an occasional deep clean, scour your boards using white vinegar.

I wasn't the kind of mother who asked her kids to take their **SHOES OFF** in the house. Only when they were really muddy or dirty. When I go to PEOPLE'S HOMES and they either ask or **SUGGEST** that I take my shoes off, well, I just won't do it. That's inhospitable! What's more important—having a SPIC-AND-SPAN house or being **HOSPITABLE?**

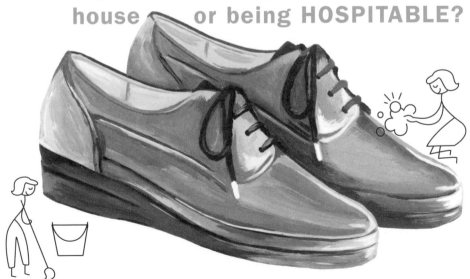

CLEANING the KITCHEN FLOORS

CARPET

Carpet in the kitchen is miserable stuff: You can never get all the dirt out. I learned my lesson—we finally put in some good linoleum. We've had it for a good many years now and it's just as beautiful as ever—and so easy to clean. Put down a different floor, that's what I say. Otherwise, vacuuming is your best bet.

CERAMIC TILE

These surfaces are so durable you don't even need a cleaner to make them sparkle; just mop them with warm water. And if you get gooey gum or wax on the floor, loosen it up with a plastic spatula and wipe up the residue with some club soda.

LAMINATE

Soap may dull the finish, so create a mixture of equal parts water and distilled white vinegar.

LINOLEUM

Just use warm water. I like to tackle my linoleum on my hands and knees so that I can really get into the corners. And if you see any black scuff marks while you're down there (linoleum tends to show them), get at them with a pencil eraser and some elbow grease.

SEALED HARDWOOD

These hardly need any care; you can just use a mop dampened with water and all-purpose cleaning liquid.

UNSEALED HARDWOOD

These are another story. Don't use water, because it can cause the floors to warp or stain. About every two weeks, apply a layer of raw linseed or jojoba oil, then go over the surface with a dry mop.

VINYL

Mop with a solution of one cup distilled white vinegar to two gallons warm water.

GETTING CANNY ABOUT CANNING

All that gardening I did (and still do!) meant that come summer, we enjoyed a real bounty of corn, beans, pickles, apples, rhubarb—you name it, I grew it. Foods fresh from the garden are delicious, but even a family of eleven couldn't polish off all those fruits and vegetables. Canning is a way to enjoy the taste of summer all year long.

Years ago I bought a large pressure cooker at a garage sale for five dollars. You can find them almost anywhere. You don't need a pressure cooker, but I think it's the easiest and fastest way. Each type has a different set of directions, so read yours carefully. Since everyone I know tends to get overrun with tomatoes, I've given you instructions on canning whole tomatoes.

WHAT YOU NEED

21 tomatoes (about twenty pounds), grown fresh from the garden (3 large tomatoes for every 1 quart jar)

½ cup lemon juice

1 quart water

1 pressure cooker

1 large pot for the tomatoes

1 medium-size pot to heat the water added to the jars

1 small pot to sterilize the lids

7 quart jars

Lids (thin, flat, round metal ones with a gum binder; they may be used only once.)

Rings (metal bands that secure the lids to the jars; they may be reused many times.)

Large spoons and ladles

Lots of clean cloths and soap for cleanup afterwards

1 First, get yourself some jars, like Ball jars. For twenty pounds of tomatoes, you'll need the equivalent of seven quarts.

2 Clean your jars in hot, soapy water. Run your hands along the jars to make sure there are no cracks or chips. Even the tiniest chip can mean the jar will break during the canning process.

3 Put the jars in the dishwasher to sterilize them. No dishwasher? Boil water and pour it into each jar. Then rinse the jars out. Sterile and perfect.

4 Now it's time to sterilize the lids and bands in boiling water. Just pop the lids and bands into a pot of water, bring the water to a boil, and keep them at a simmer until you're ready to put the lids on. Use tongs to lift the lids out so that you don't burn your hands. (You can also use the "sterilize" setting on your dishwasher, then place them in a pan of hot water until you need them.)

5 To remove the tomato skins, wash the tomatoes and dip them in boiling water for thirty to sixty seconds or until the skins begin to split. Then blanch them in an ice-water bath, slipping off the skins and the core. Remove any discolored parts.

6 Put the tomatoes into the jar, leaving about half an inch of space on top. Add two tablespoons of lemon juice, which helps to minimize spoilage and retains color and flavor to boot. Then pour boiling water in until you reach half an inch of the top.

7 Slide a wooden spoon up and down the edges of the jar to release any air bubbles.

8 Be absolutely certain the rims of the jars are clean before you put the lids on. Even a stray seed can mean you don't get a good seal. After you've wiped the rims clean, remove your lids and bands from the pot and seal your jars. Make sure they're sealed very tightly!

9 Carefully place the jars in a warm-water bath in the pressure cooker. Put on the pressure cooker's big, heavy lid, locking down the sides.

10 Let the steam escape really well, then close the valve to build up pressure. Wait for the gauge to pop up and then set the jars aside. Repeat until you're out of tomatoes (or jars!).

11 Label the jars and store them in a dark, cool, and dry area (I like to use my crawl space). Enjoy your wonderful tomatoes all winter long.

2 NEW BAKERS in my KITCHEN

Some of my sweetest memories take place in the kitchen. And more often than not, those fond memories are of the messes that come with kids and cooking.

Monica and Maria, my two oldest daughters, were just big enough to hold spoons when I taught them to bake. It was a rainy Saturday afternoon in early May—I remember it was thundering so hard that Maria kept singing "It's firecrackers, firecrackers, firecrackers!" Since the girls were stuck inside, we needed a good activity. I thought I'd teach my four- and five-year-old how to bake. We decided to make chocolate-chip cookies with nuts and oatmeal, because they're healthier that way. And the kids just loved them.

The three of us gathered around the pink linoleum counter, me in my long floral apron and the girls in clothes that I had made for them. Monica wore the most adorable pants—a pair of corduroys sewn from blue, yellow, and red scraps. I had sewn suspenders right on—you know, so they'd stay up and not fall down like lots of elastic-waist pants seem to do. Maria wore little light-blue denim pants and a matching pullover shirt with denim ribbons that tied at the neck in a bow. I got off on the right foot with mess insurance by grabbing two tea towels from the pantry, wrapping them around the girls' waists, and pinning them in the back with clothespins.

The girls were jumping up and down when I took my mixer out of the cupboard. It was a big white Oster one, with a glass bowl. Their eyes got really wide. They couldn't see the top of the counter, so I stood them on kitchen chairs for a better view. They started playing with the switches on the mixer, running it slow, fast, turning it on and off, before there was even anything in the bowl. That should've been a red flag right there!

We started with the flour. Maria put the red plastic measuring cup in the flour jar and filled it up, and then I put Monica's hand in mine and we leveled the flour with a butter knife. So far so good.

When we got to the eggs, though, things got messy. I showed the girls how to gently crack an egg on the side of the bowl and then use their fingers to pull the shell apart. But why crack an egg gently, they thought, when you can slam it into the side of the bowl? Sheesh.

And they were quick to take a taste, I'll tell you that. Every time I turned my back to get a new egg or an ingredient from the cupboard, they'd put their little fingers inside the bowl or run them down the sides of the beaters to sneak a lick. But they soon learned to taste the dough when it was good and ready, not before all the sugar was creamed into it! They must have tried it with just baking soda and salt in there, because I turned around to see Maria spitting a mouthful into the sink and Monica's face twisted in disgusted surprise.

When it was time to chop the nuts, I grabbed this little metal turn-crank nutcracker out of the drawer. Maria and Monica fought over who would use it first. I let Monica start, since Maria had cracked the last egg.

After all the ingredients were in and I let them have a hand at the mixer, it was time for the grand finale of mess making. The girls lifted the beaters out of the dough while they were spinning, and flour, salt, sugar, and eggs went just about everywhere! Truly, weeks later I was still finding cookie goop in little crevices. What a mess that was. Delicious cookies, though.

CHAPTER 2

a clean
BATHROOM

The bathroom is for all those **GOOD THINGS** like taking a shower, combing your hair, and putting on makeup. ⟹

Well, the makeup part doesn't really apply to me. Or at least it didn't when the kids were young—I just never had time for it. Come to think of it, I didn't always have time for daily showers back then either. It's important to have a nice, clean place to get ready for the day—or to clean up after a long, hard day—in peace. So I try to keep my bathrooms as clean as possible, because I don't like dirty toilets one bit. Who does?

When it comes to bathrooms, I say the smaller the better. It's fairly easy for me to keep mine spic-and-span, because it's nice and compact. I know a lot of people are putting in really big bathrooms today, and I just don't get it at all; to me, it's a waste of products, energy, and time. My tiny bathroom suits me just fine—I'm able to clean the whole floor on my hands and knees!

One thing that's changed for the better with the times is cleaning supplies. Fifty years ago—even just ten years ago—you used bleach and products with harsh chemicals to clean the bathroom. If it didn't have a strong bleach smell, then it wasn't clean. Now I clean entirely without bleach. I have to admit it's a delight to use something that smells good while I clean, and to not feel dizzy from the harsh chemicals. If only some of these products had been around when I had nine kids under one roof!

the SHOWER 67

making GLASS SHOWER DOORS shine 67

cleaning FIBERGLASS WALLS 67

treating TILES to a RUBDOWN 67

cleaning SHOWER TRACKS, FRAMES, and RODS 68

removing MILDEW from CAULK 68

scouring SHOWER CURTAINS 68

getting MINERAL DEPOSITS off the SHOWERHEAD 68

getting into those GROUT LINES 68

the MIRROR 69

making the MIRROR SPARKLE 69

cleaning up BROKEN GLASS 69

getting HAIRSPRAY and TOOTHPASTE off a MIRROR 69

the CABINETS 71

cleaning WOODEN CABINETS 71

making the MEDICINE CABINET LOOK LIKE NEW 71

the TOILET 71

tackling the TOILET 71

getting RUST STAINS off the TOILET 71

cleaning the TOILET SEAT 71

the **TUB** 72

tackling the TUB 72

attacking the RING around the TUB 72

cleaning NONSLIP DECALS 72

UNCLOGGING the DRAIN 72

REPLACING CAULK 72

the **FLOORS** 73

MOPPING UP the FLOORS 73

buffing BATHROOM FLOORS 74

the **SINK** 76

making your SINKS SPARKLE 76

getting out MINERAL STAINS 76

shining the FAUCETS and FIXTURES 77

the **ATMOSPHERE** 78

WARMING UP the BATHROOM 78

keeping the BATHROOM SMELLING FRESH 78

VENTILATING the BATHROOM 78

FANNING your BATHROOM 78

keeping the BATHROOM SAFE 79

performing bathroom TRIAGE 80

TOOLBOX

BRUSHES
Nylon bristle
Toilet
Toothbrush

BUCKETS, GLOVES, and MORE
Bucket or pail
Spray bottle

CLEANING PRODUCTS
All-purpose cleaning liquid
Baby wipes
Baking soda
Club soda
Cola
Cream of tartar
Denture tablets
Dishwashing liquid
Hydrogen peroxide
Rubbing alcohol
Shampoo
Shaving cream
Surface spray
White vinegar

CLOTHS, RAGS, SPONGES, and OTHER WIPERS
Cloth
Cotton balls
Newspaper
Old nylon stockings
Rag
Squeegee

SWEEPING, MOPPING, and VACUUMING
Broom
Mop
Sponge
Vacuum
with attachments

ODOR FIXERS
Eucalyptus oil
Lemon juice

STAIN REMOVAL
Oxygen bleach

HANDY to HAVE THESE AROUND
Hairdryer
Pumice stone
Salt
Toothpick or straight pin

the SHOWER

Making Glass Shower Doors Shine

Go to the hardware store and get a squeegee—yup, like the ones gas-station attendants use—and squeegee those doors with equal parts white vinegar and water after every shower. You'll never have to do a big clean. Just fill a spray bottle and keep it right there on the shower ledge. When you get out of the shower, leave the door open a crack to let air in and curb mildew buildup.

Cleaning Fiberglass Walls

Just wipe down the walls with a squeegee or an inexpensive towel after every bath or shower. Go from top to bottom, and if you keep it up, you will save hours and hours of cleaning time. If you see water spots, you may have hard water. Since hard water can be such a bear, I recommend getting yourself a water conditioner or softener. Vern made every bit of our fiberglass shower, which was in the kids' bathroom. I hadn't ever showered in that bathroom until recently, when we were renovating our bathroom. It was so small that when I dropped a bar of soap, I bumped my head—and my butt! I had no idea how tiny it was. Our kids never once complained.

Treating Tiles to a Rubdown

GLAZED CERAMIC: Do as I do and clean the tiles right after you take a shower. It's a great time to do it, because the steam has already loosened the dirt and soap scum for you. Spritz the walls from your spray bottle filled with one part white vinegar to two parts water. Then wipe down the walls from top to bottom with a damp cloth. Whatever you do, don't use soap—it can leave a film over time.

UNGLAZED CERAMIC: Because these tiles don't have a glossy surface, you'll need a more abrasive product to get off scuffs and other marks. Mix a little baking soda (about half a cup) into a pail of warm water, and wipe the walls down from top to bottom. The soda is just a bit abrasive—great for getting off that grime.

ah, the MEMORIES

"Showers weren't exactly **RELAXING** in our house. You had to take a **QUICK** shower—I mean really quick—unless you wanted to get a headache from someone pounding on the **BATHROOM DOOR** to get you moving."

— Pat (No. 8)

Cleaning Shower Tracks, Frames, and Rods

To get annoying water marks off a metal track, frame, and shower rod, dip a toothbrush in lemon juice and scrub away. If you want to go a step further, buff the areas afterward with a dry towel.

vinegar and water for a few hours. The acidic vinegar works as a solvent—perfect for those pesky hard-water stains. Use a toothpick or straight pin to loosen any deposits in those holes.

LIFE'S LITTLE ANNOYANCES

REMOVING MILDEW FROM CAULK

The place where the wall meets the tub can be tricky to get into. So mix together equal parts lemon juice and baking soda to get that tile caulk nice and white. Dip cotton balls into the solution, line them up along the crevice, and let them sit there for a few minutes. Then wipe the area clean with a cloth.

Scouring Shower Curtains

These attract mold and mildew like crazy. So shake them out after you take a shower to get off all that extra water, then close them to air them out. To get rid of mildew, apply a paste of baking soda and water to the spots with a cloth, let it sit for a few minutes, then wipe the curtain clean with a cloth soaked in lemon juice. Or you can wash your curtains in the washer. You can put cloth curtains in the dryer; toss plastic ones in there just for a few minutes before hanging them on the line to fully dry. Don't leave them in the dryer, however—the plastic will melt!

Getting Mineral Deposits off the Showerhead

When calcium and lime do a number on your showerhead, take it off and soak it in the bathroom sink with equal parts white

Getting into Those Grout Lines

Dip an old toothbrush into a mixture of equal parts oxygen bleach and water and scrub, scrub, scrub until the lines get really bright. When you're done, soak the toothbrush in hydrogen peroxide so that it's clean for next time. If company's coming

WASTE NOT WANT NOT

Limiting your shower time will save water and money, but you should also consider installing a low-flow showerhead, which mixes air into the water stream, cutting down both your water and energy use by half. It only costs about ten dollars at the hardware store and can save you buckets.

and you need a quick spruce-up, light a scented candle and keep the overhead light off—it'll be dim enough that guests won't even notice the grout.

the MIRROR

Making the Mirror Sparkle

It tends to get dirty—especially right after you floss. That's my pet peeve: particles of food all over my bathroom mirror! To get the mirror shiny and looking like new, fill a spray bottle with club soda and give it a spritz, then wipe it really well with bunched-up newspaper. To defog the mirror so that you can see your pretty face the second you step out of the shower, smear the glass with a bit of shaving cream and then wipe it off—or point the hairdryer at it for a minute or two.

Cleaning Up Broken Glass

If a mirror falls on a tile floor, you may get seven years of bad luck—and you'll definitely get little shards all over the place. To make sure you remove all those pieces, dab a piece of bread on top of them. (Yes, white bread will grab some of those small, sharp pieces.) Vacuum, then wipe down the floor with a water-dampened cloth. Be very careful when you wring it out.

GETTING **HAIRSPRAY** and **TOOTHPASTE** off a **MIRROR**

Pour rubbing alcohol on a cloth and clean in small circles. You can also use a baby wipe, if you have one of those handy. Then grab your club-soda spray bottle and give the mirror a spritz, wiping it clean with some bunched-up newspaper.

the CABINETS

Cleaning Wooden Cabinets

Wipe these down with a damp cloth and a squirt of dishwashing liquid. Then dry them right away so they won't warp or streak.

Making the Medicine Cabinet Look Like New

Every month or so, take out your goodies and wipe down those shelves with warm water and dishwashing liquid. Then, before you put all your toiletries back in, weed out things you haven't used since the Reagan administration. This might surprise you, but please don't keep medicines in here—they should be stored in a cool, dry place so that they retain maximum potency. The bathroom is way too hot and humid for medicine.

Take note of how long you've had your makeup, too. I learned a lot about makeup by having four teenage girls around: Mascara lasts only three months, and it's important that you remember when you opened it, because that wand gets a build-up of bacteria that you don't want going in your eyes. Sunscreen lasts one year and lipstick up to three. If you have trouble keeping track of how old things are, start writing the dates on them with a permanent marker when they're new. Remember this piece of advice: If you can't remember when you bought it, throw it out!

the TOILET

Tackling the Toilet

Sometimes you get a ring in there that you just can't get out. Try this: Pour in half a cup of distilled white vinegar and let it sit for a few hours or even overnight before giving the bowl a swipe with the toilet brush. You have to be careful to flush your toilets after every use—Vern and I always are. But the kids when they were young? Not so much. When it gets really bad, toss some denture tablets down there. Let them sit and foam for about five minutes, then scrub the spots with a toilet brush. When the inside's clean, wipe the exterior with a cloth dipped in warm water and all-purpose cleaner, then put that cloth in the laundry right away—it will have bacteria on it that you don't want to get on anything else.

Getting Rust Stains off the Toilet

For truly tough rust stains, which are caused by the iron in water, pour a can of cola into the bowl and let it sit overnight. The soda will disintegrate the rust so you can wipe the bowl clean with a toilet brush.

Cleaning the Toilet Seat

Whether you have plastic, porcelain, or wooden seats, wipe them down with all-purpose cleaning liquid and warm water. And dry them thoroughly—you don't want a damp bottom.

the TUB

Tackling the Tub

Cleaning the tub is a lot of work! The best thing to do is wipe it down after each bath and shower so that soap scum won't build up. To scour it, sprinkle baking soda around and then use a nylon-bristle brush and warm water. And don't forget the rubber tub stopper—that attracts mold and mildew like nobody's business, so scrub it well with dishwashing liquid.

Attacking the Ring around the Tub

Use a pair of old nylon stockings as your cloth to rub that ring of mineral deposits away. Since the stockings are gently abrasive, you probably won't even need to use soap. For more stubborn stains, mix together equal parts salt and white vinegar, spread the paste on the spots, and let it sit for an hour or two before wiping it up with warm water.

Cleaning Nonslip Decals

Those decals on the bottom of your tub get dirty, all right, and then they become slippery, defeating their purpose. Sprinkle some baking soda on them and scrub with a toothbrush and water.

Unclogging the Drain

Drains get clogged by everything from hair to the oils in your soaps and shampoos. So once every two or three months, pour half a cup of baking soda and then half a cup of white vinegar down there. After a few minutes, boil some water in your teakettle and pour it down the drain.

REPLACING CAULK

If you see any caulk coming loose—between the walls of the shower and the tub, for instance—it's important to fix it so that moisture doesn't get into the walls and cause major damage. Here's what you do: Use a utility knife to carefully cut the old caulk away. Clean the gap that's left with soapy water and dry it thoroughly. Then squeeze a nice line of water-based caulk (you can get it at the hardware store) along the seam, using the back of a plastic spoon to smooth it as you go. After the caulk dries, trim any excess with a razor blade.

MOPPING UP THE FLOORS

I won't say that there's a right and wrong way to mop, but there are ways to make mopping more efficient.

1 First, make sure you have a dry floor, because if you vacuum or sweep any wetness around, you're just spreading out your mess.

2 Sweep or vacuum your floor thoroughly. The bathroom is especially apt to accumulate a lot of hair, grit, and what have you. Get it all out of there!

3 Fill your bucket with warm water and just a little bit of all-purpose cleaning solution. Remember, using more than the directions indicate doesn't mean you'll get your floor any cleaner! In fact, too much soap can leave residue.

4 Wring out your mop thoroughly. A damp mop lifts dirt; a soaked mop just swishes it around.

5 Start in the farthest corner of the room and work your way toward the door. After I mopped myself into a corner once, I learned my lesson.

6 Use back-and-forth strokes as you go. Make two passes on every part of the floor. After several passes, dip your mop into the bucket, wring it out, and keep going. When that water gets murky, fill it with fresh cleaning solution and water.

7 You're not going to be able to get the mop into every nook and cranny, mind you. Tight corners mean immersing a cloth in your bucket and wringing it out until it's just damp, then getting down on your hands and knees to tackle those corners and crevices.

8 When you're finished, go back over the room with clean, warm water and a damp mop. Then take a step back, admire your work, and enjoy your bright, shiny bathroom floors!

BUFFING BATHROOM FLOORS

Whether you have laminate or something newfangled like recycled glass, clean bathroom floors are calming, especially for those who need a ten-minute escape from a houseful of kids! Here's how to make these surfaces shine.

CERAMIC TILE, GLAZED	Ground-in dirt can scratch these shiny tiles in no time, so before you even get to mopping, vacuum the floor, using the crevice attachment to get into the corners. Then mop with a solution of one gallon water to one tablespoon rubbing alcohol.
CERAMIC TILE, UNGLAZED	Vacuum thoroughly, then mop with all-purpose cleaning liquid and water. Avoid regular use of acidic cleaners here (like white vinegar), which can cause discoloration.
LAMINATE	This type of flooring, which is made to look like different materials, from stone to tile to wood, needs to be vacuumed then mopped with a solution of one tablespoon white vinegar to one gallon of water.
LINOLEUM	Your grandmother probably had linoleum. And maybe even your grandmother's mother, too. It's an all-natural, super-durable flooring material made of linseed oil, limestone, resins, and wood powder. To clean it, pick up excess dust with a dust mop. Add a few squirts of all-purpose cleaning liquid to a gallon of water, and mop—trying not to get seams and edges too wet, or else they may loosen.

RECYCLED GLASS

These tiles, made from things like old glass bottles, don't need much care. Just mop with warm water and all-purpose cleaning liquid.

STONE (LIMESTONE, MARBLE, AND SLATE)

Sweep or vacuum regularly to minimize ground-in dirt. Heavily dilute all-purpose cleaning liquid in warm water and wring your mop out until it's damp. If you have a deep-set stain, try a stone poultice.

VINYL

There are so many choices of vinyl floors today—from an endless array of colors to vinyl made to look like wood, tile, or stone. Place floor protectors under heavy furniture to minimize indentations. Mop with all-purpose cleaning liquid and water.

THE BEST MOP FOR THE JOB

DUST MOP
A must-have for dust and cobwebs.

RAG MOP
Your go-to tool for large bathrooms—it covers a lot of ground.

SPONGE MOP
Great for wet mopping and lightweight too!

MAKING YOUR SINKS SPARKLE

Wipe down your sink with a cloth after every use to prevent soap-scum buildup as well as the formation of stains from lime and other mineral deposits. It'll make your weekly cleaning easier. To tackle various types of sinks, follow this advice:

PORCELAIN

Apply a mixture of equal parts cream of tartar and hydrogen peroxide with a soft rag. Let it sit there for an hour before wiping it up.

ACRYLIC

Wipe down with all-purpose cleaning liquid and warm water. Finish with white vinegar to disinfect it further.

LIMESTONE, MARBLE, and GRANITE

You never want to use anything abrasive on stone or else you might scratch it. And stay away from vinegar, too—it can penetrate the surface layer, causing damage. Instead, dampen a soft cloth with water and dishwashing liquid and clean in small circles. Rinse with a clean cloth and water. Get out marble stains by applying a poultice.

SOLID SURFACE

Sold under brand names including Corian, Avonite, and Samsung Staron, solid-surface sinks are pretty hardy. If yours has a glossy finish, clean with a solution of equal parts white vinegar and water. If it has a matte (dull) finish, wipe it down with dishwashing liquid and water, then again with a clean cloth dampened in water.

getting out
MINERAL STAINS

A dripping faucet can often leave brown mineral stains in the sink. To get them out, sprinkle salt on the area and rub it in with distilled white vinegar.

SHINING the
FAUCETS and FIXTURES

Got TOOTHPASTE dripping down the side of the sink? Dab it up with a CLOTH and RUB IT ON your sink and shower faucets to BRIGHTEN them up.

the ATMOSPHERE

Warming Up the Bathroom

One thing I like having in the bathroom is a ceiling heater. It warms you when you get out of the shower. When it's chilly, you just flip a switch and the room heats up fast. And it's better than wasting energy to overheat the entire house just because you're cold from your shower.

Keeping the Bathroom Smelling Fresh

Fill a spray bottle with water, three drops of lemon oil, and two drops of eucalyptus oil. Shake this really well before using.

Ventilating the Bathroom

Mold and mildew form when there's not enough air circulation. When moisture builds up, mold and mildew will grow on the walls. Eventually, you'll get some blistering and peeling on the paint or wallpaper. So keep the window open when you shower to release excess steam from the room. No window? Keep the door open while you shower, if you can, or just open it when you're done.

Fanning Your Bathroom

For those of you without windows, I suggest getting a bathroom fan installed. The initial cost of a fan will save you money in the long term: Mildew and mold, once in the tiles, can be expensive to fix, and a fan really improves ventilation. To clean the fan, first turn off the bathroom's power via the fuse box or circuit breaker. Remove the cover, unplug the fan, and pull it out. Take a dry cloth and sweep the dust from the cover and the fan itself. Vacuum the fan, then wipe it with a damp cloth. Once it's dry, replace the fan and re-cover it. If, however, the cover is very dirty, a good hot soak in soapy water and a scrub should get it clean. Let it dry thoroughly before placing it back on.

WASTE NOT WANT NOT

Stop throwing out those little pieces of soap! It's valuable stuff! Take the soap chips from all the sinks and showers in your house and put them in a big plastic jug under the kitchen sink with a little water so they don't dry out. When the jug gets full, set it in a pan on the stove with a little water and heat it very, very slowly, stirring, until all the soap melts. You can use that melted-down soap in the washing machine to tackle greasy jeans!

KEEPING the BATHROOM SAFE

Having nine kids meant that the house stayed childproofed for nearly twenty years. In addition to keeping medicine out of the way of little hands by storing it elsewhere, here are other precautions you can take to make the bathroom safe for your family:

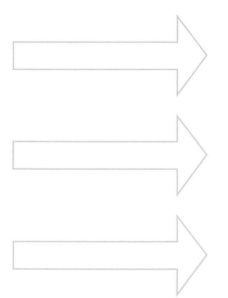

Use a rubber mat with suction cups in the tub to prevent falls. Scrub it with hot, soapy water and hang to dry weekly to avoid mildew growth. Or better yet, try those antislip adhesives. Once a week, just sprinkle some baking soda on them and scrub with a toothbrush and water.

Keep hairdryers, curling irons, and any other electrical products away from sinks and tubs.

Place bath mats on the floor in front of the tub and sink to help keep it dry. Watery floors mean slippery floors!

PERFORMING BATHROOM TRIAGE

As a nurse, I always taught my kids to be prepared in an emergency. Do the same: Post emergency phone numbers someplace convenient and keep a list of each child's allergies right near it. And make sure that at least one bathroom in your home is equipped with a first-aid kit. You can buy a prepackaged one, but it's just as easy to use this handy checklist to assemble your own.

ACTIVATED-CHARCOAL SOLUTION TO ABSORB CAUSTIC POISONS
do not use before calling either the poison control center or 911

ADHESIVE BANDAGES (assorted sizes)

ADHESIVE TAPE and MASKING TAPE

ANTIBIOTIC CREAM

ANTIHISTAMINE

ANTISEPTIC CLEANSING WIPES/SPRAY

BLANKET

BURN OINTMENT

CALAMINE LOTION

CHEMICAL COLD PACK

COTTON BALLS

COTTON SWABS

DISPOSABLE GLOVES

ELASTIC BANDAGES

EYEWASH SOLUTION

FEVER REDUCERS and PAIN MEDICATIONS (over-the-counter) FOR BOTH ADULTS AND CHILDREN

FLASHLIGHT AND BATTERIES

FIRST-AID POCKET GUIDE

GAUZE (ROLLS AND PADS)

HAND CLEANER

HYDROGEN PEROXIDE

PLASTIC BAGS

RUBBING ALCOHOL

SAFETY PINS

SCISSORS

THERMOMETER

TRIANGULAR BANDAGES

TWEEZERS

THE **BATHROOM** is YOUR HOME'S **E.R.**

I'm a trained nurse who's seen her share of accidents, and I can tell you that some of the real doozies happened right here at home. My bathroom was always well stocked with supplies: bandages, antibiotic salves, thermometers, cotton balls—and luckily, tweezers. Carrying a crying child to the bathroom and bandaging an injury is just part of being a mother. Performing a carrot-ectomy, however, is a rare occasion.

The carrot episode involved Pat, who was a very calm, shy child. I never had to tell him to go to sleep—he was in bed right at eight o'clock every night. Not a troublemaker or a tantrum-thrower. But boy, did he get himself into a pickle when he was eight years old.

It was fall, so I decided to make a nice stew for dinner—with meat and potatoes and peas and carrots. I sent Pat outside to dig up some carrots from the garden. He wasn't too happy about it, as he wanted to continue playing ping-pong. But he went ahead and did it.

Ten minutes later, I heard hysterical screaming: "Mom . . . carrot . . . finger!" I ran to the door to meet him. "Mom!" Pant, pant, pant. "I got a carrot down my finger!" Sure enough, the middle finger of his right hand had a big piece of bright-orange carrot stuck halfway underneath the fingernail. Was that a sight to be seen! I was about to hoist him up onto the countertop to get a better look, but then all of a sudden he just flopped down on the linoleum floor like a rag doll. He'd fainted!

Now that Pat was out cold, I could perform minor surgery with no anesthetic. I lifted him up and ran him over to the bathroom. "Quick, grab the tweezers," I said to Pat's big brother Joe. "I need to pull this carrot out while he's out!" Joe handed me the tweezers, then stood over me while I grabbed the carrot. It was a clean procedure: The carrot came out in one piece. Phew! When the poor little guy came to, he was surprised that it wasn't there anymore. I washed and bandaged his finger and gave it a little kiss. Good as new. As for the stew, it was still quite delicious, I must say. Even without the carrots.

CHAPTER 3

a clean
LIVING ROOM

In my opinion, a living room should have comfy seating and a place to rest a cup of coffee or tea. My living room is for living. But when I was a girl, our living room was blocked off—only company could go in there, not us. So I've always made sure to set up my own living room with comfort in mind. Case in point: Vern and I have had these two recliners for years, but they didn't swivel, so they just weren't conducive to conversation. $\Longrightarrow$

One day we went to Goodwill and saw two swivel chairs for only $5 each! Vern said to the clerk, "We'll take the swivel parts off and leave the rest of the chairs here." So that's what we did. He got a screwdriver, took off those swivel apparatuses, and attached them to our recliners. I've also learned to buy upholstery that doesn't show dirt. Prints like florals or textures like tweeds, are great for this. And watch out for coffee tables with sharp edges. When the kids were growing up, we had two blond-wood coffee tables with very sharp edges, and I remember the kids falling and hitting their heads all the time after bouts of roughhousing.

Our upstairs family room was also designed as a place where we could all relax. It was done up with dark paneling and gold-painted walls, beams across the ceiling, lots of cupboards, and a wet bar with a fridge and a sink. In that room I taught Tom, Tim, Joe, Pat, and Dan to play ping-pong—though when they improved and learned how to spike that ball, I had to duck out. (I still have dings in my cupboards from when they'd swing their paddles!) That's also the room Maria would sneak into to talk on the phone with her boyfriend. Vern would have a fit when he couldn't get through because the line was busy.

The family room is where I hosted my bridge club. I'd serve homemade dessert and soda, tea, or coffee for the girls. And there would always be nuts and candy left up there, so if the kids knew I'd had bridge, why, they were right up the stairs the next morning to see what goodies they could find. Of course, the first ones up there got it all. They sure looked forward to that, because I never had that stuff in the house any other time.

the FLOORS 89

VACUUMING the CARPET 89

caring for WOOD FLOORS 89

WAXING WOOD FLOORS 90

FLOOR DISORDER 90

cleaning SEALED HARDWOOD FLOORS 90

cleaning UNSEALED HARDWOOD FLOORS 90

SPOT WAXING SCUFF MARKS 90

taking care of BAMBOO FLOORS 90

cleaning the RUGS 91

the WALLS 92

washing the WALLS 92

removing CRAYON from WALLS 92

dealing with the DRAPES 92

cleaning METAL, VINYL, OR WOOD BLINDS 93

finessing FABRIC SHADES 93

the CEILINGS 93

dusting the CEILINGS 93

scrubbing ACOUSTIC TILE 93

picking your CEILING PAINT 93

the LIGHT FIXTURES 95

getting LIGHT FIXTURES to SHINE 95

dusting PLEATED LAMP SHADES 95

dusting FLAT SHADES 95

washing LAMP SHADES 95

the ACCESSORIES 96

cleaning BRASS CANDLESTICKS 96

dusting HOUSEPLANTS 96

dealing with BRASS or COPPER DOORKNOBS 96

cleaning FRAMES 96

fixing up the FIREPLACE 97

cleaning BRASS, CAST-IRON, or WROUGHT-IRON SCREENS, ANDIRONS, and TOOLS 97

the ENTERTAINMENT 98

battling the BOOB TUBE 98

disinfecting the REMOTE 98

sprucing up the SPEAKERS 98

dusting other ELECTRONICS 98

prettying up the PIANO 98

the FURNITURE 100

cleaning UPHOLSTERED SOFAS, CHAIRS, and OTTOMANS 100

REMOVING STAINS from UPHOLSTERED FURNITURE 101

cleaning NON-UPHOLSTERED FURNITURE 102

WAXING WOOD FURNITURE 103

PETS on the PREMISES 104

TRICKS of the TRADE 105

TOOLBOX

BRUSHES
Paintbrush
Stiff brush
Toothbrush

BUCKETS, GLOVES, and MORE
Bucket or pail
Rubber gloves
Spray bottle

CLEANING PRODUCTS
All-purpose
cleaning liquid
Baking soda
Countertop spray
Dishwashing liquid
Distilled water
Glass cleaner
Laundry detergent
Mild soap
Rubbing alcohol
Solvent cleaner
White vinegar
Window spray

CLOTHS, RAGS, SPONGES, and OTHER WIPERS
Chamois
Cloth
Cotton balls
Dry sponge
Extendable duster
Feather duster
Microfiber cloth
Muslin
Newspaper
Rag
Sponge
Steel wool

SWEEPING, MOPPING, and VACUUMING
Broom
Hand broom
Mop
Vacuum
with attachments

STAIN REMOVAL
Dry-cleaning solvent
Enzyme-based cleaner
Laundry detergent
Upholstery shampoo
White towel

WAXING and POLISHING
Furniture polish
Linseed or jojoba oil
Olive oil
Paste wax

HANDY to HAVE THESE AROUND
Can of compressed air
Fan or hairdryer
Flour
Salt
Wood crayon

the FLOORS

Vacuuming the Carpet

It's so important to vacuum your carpets at least once a week (twice, if someone in your house has allergies), because they are dirt and dust magnets. And there are a couple of things you can do to keep your carpets looking new: Close your drapes when you're not home to minimize fading, and use coasters under heavy furniture so that you don't get those pesky carpet indentations. Remember, after every vacuuming job, take off the brush attachment and vacuum it—because if you don't, it'll get so full of lint it won't pick up very well. And make sure you empty the bag. You'll lose suction if you don't keep your bag empty. I used to have red shag carpets, and I loved them—they were warm and just perfect for when the kids were playing. But they were hard to vacuum.

Caring for Wood Floors

Polyurethane has been used to finish floors since the '70s, and it really does help protect against those inevitable spills and scratches. Once floors have been polyurethaned, you don't need to wax them, that's the perk (though my kids did love to fly around on freshly waxed floors in their socks). If your floor is finished with varnish or shellac (you'll know if you scratch it with a dime and it flakes), you should wax twice a year or so.

my **HOUSE,** my **RULES**

When my twins, **TIM** and **TOM**, were three years old, they'd help me **SHINE** the wood floors in the living room. I'd apply a paste wax, and as soon as it dried, it was their turn. I'd give each of them a towel and let them **RUN** and **SLIDE** around on the floor. They'd pull each other this way and that and slip all around. They loved it! And they didn't even realize **THEY WERE CLEANING**. We didn't have much furniture at the time — a sofa, and that's about it — so there was lots of space to slide around in. Every year we would add a piece of furniture to the room. When you add children, they need **PLACES TO SIT!**

Waxing Wood Floors

Before you do anything, vacuum and dust your floors. Wax unsealed hardwood floors with paste wax formulated for wood floors. Apply the wax directly—as thinly as possible—and spread it with a clean cloth. Let it dry for fifteen to thirty minutes. You can buff the floors by hand with a fresh, clean cloth, but who has the time? Instead, rent a buffing machine from the hardware store or do as I did: Have your kids each take a clean cloth and rub that wax right off. A second coat isn't necessary, but if you want that gorgeous shine, it might be worth it to you.

Cleaning Unsealed Hardwood Floors

Vacuum these floors every week. Once a month apply a layer of raw linseed or jojoba oil, then go over the surface with a dry mop. It's very important that you don't get these floors wet, or they will warp in no time flat.

Spot Waxing Scuff Marks

Heel marks, scuffs, and the like are going to happen, but I still don't force people to take their shoes off. A quick spot wax is easy enough: Rub the mark with a little paste floor wax and steel wool, let dry, then buff. Gone in a flash.

FLOOR DISORDER

Have you ever rearranged your furniture only to find indentations in your carpet or area rug? Rub the marks with ice cubes; as the carpet fibers absorb the water, they'll swell back into shape. Blot the area with a dry towel, then vacuum. If you see a scratch on your wood floor, get a crayon of a similar color and fill it in. To prevent scratching in the future, place felt pads underneath your furnishings.

Cleaning Sealed Hardwood Floors

By sealed floors, I mean those treated with all urethane, polyurethane, polyacrylic, and water-based finishes. Sweep or vacuum these every week. They hardly need any care; you can just use a damp mop with a little all-purpose cleaning liquid and water. Steer clear of vinegar here; it may cause your floors to dull over time.

Taking Care of Bamboo Floors

Bamboo is part of the grass family and it's getting more and more popular because while trees can take decades to grow back, bamboo grows much more quickly—it replenishes itself in only four years! Good for Mother Earth. Typically, bamboo floors are sealed, so they require the same care as sealed hardwood floors: A damp mop with some all-purpose cleaner and water should do the trick.

Cleaning the Rugs

My children still tease me about our thick red shag carpet. I loved it, but they say they lost valuables in there. The truth is, rugs collect a lot of grit and dirt. So about once a month, take your rugs outside and shake them out. Vacuuming weekly isn't enough; once a year you'll need to do a deep clean. You can rent a steam cleaner for many rugs, though most Oriental rugs should be cleaned by a professional. And make sure to spot clean your rugs regularly. You can make your own spot remover by diluting a quarter teaspoon of clear dishwashing liquid in one quart of water.

JUTE, COIR, HEMP, AND SISAL: For these, steam cleaning won't work. You'll need to rent a dry-extraction machine at the hardware store. These rugs are hard to keep clean, so relegate them to low-traffic areas. Blot spills with your homemade spot remover (see above), and dry damp areas quickly by using a fan or a hairdryer on low heat.

SYNTHETIC: Vacuum thoroughly, then use a shampooing and steam-cleaning machine. Blot any stains with a clean, white cloth and a spot remover (see above).

WOOL: You'll need to have wool rugs professionally cleaned because rental steam cleaners can leave too much water, making carpets vulnerable to damage. Blot—don't rub—stains with tepid water and a clean, white towel. (Colored towels will worsen the stain.)

my **HOUSE,** my **RULES**

Eating only in the **KITCHEN** and **DINING ROOM** is essential to keeping a tidy home. I was always pretty strict about this rule: **NO EATING IN THE LIVING ROOM!** But even though all the kids knew not to bring their oatmeal cookies in there, I'd inevitably catch someone nibbling on something while sitting on the sofa, and I'd have to tell him or her to move it on over to the **KITCHEN TABLE.** You don't want to tell your kids to do something that you can't enforce, though, so I made sure that if I instructed them to sit at the table, I had a clear view of it and **I COULD SEE** whether they were really doing it.

the WALLS

Washing the Walls

The best trick for keeping your walls clean is to tell children to stop touching them. Short of that, spot cleaning is the way to go. Wet a cloth with some all-purpose cleaning liquid and water and scrub. Since walls in the really-lived-in rooms can get so dirty, however, it might be worth your while to do a big wall cleaning every two years or when they start to look dingy all around. First remove your window treatments or pull up the blinds. Clear the knickknacks off the counters, and of course remove any art from the walls. Then vacuum the walls, using the attachment. When you're ready, dilute all-purpose cleaning liquid in water and use a sponge mop, starting from the top of the wall and moving down. Rinse the mop frequently, and get into the hard-to-reach crevices and the baseboards with a sponge. Then dry the wall with a clean cloth attached to a mop.

Removing Crayon from Walls

If there's a mother who hasn't had to remove crayon from the wall at some point, I haven't met her. Basically, getting crayon out, whether it's on paint or wallpaper, requires a lot of muscle. Dilute a few drops of dishwashing liquid in warm water, wet your cloth, and get to work scrubbing. Rinse the cloth frequently, and when the water starts to get murky looking, clean out the pail and start the process again until the wall is crayon-free. As for preventing such messes in the future, two things: Explain (again) that coloring is for paper only, and cover your walls with a glossy paint. Much easier to wipe clean.

Dealing with the Drapes

If your drapes look clean, you'll hardly ever need to wash them in the machine; just hang them out on the line about twice a year to air them out. I had fiberglass drapes for years—fiberglass is synthetic, so they never faded. And I never washed them, not once, because those fibers would get all nasty in a washing machine. Now I have swing-back cotton curtains with a scalloped valance on the top. Beautiful teal, lined with maroon. Teresa helped me make them—she's a great seamstress. Every spring, vacuum your drapes using the drapery attachment. If they're covered with fingerprints, you can wash them in the machine in cold water, then hang them to dry. But if they're fancy, you might want to send them out to a professional and save yourself the trouble.

Cleaning Metal, Vinyl, or Wood Blinds

Once a month, close the blinds and dust them with a barely damp cloth (or use your vacuum's attachment). Close them in the opposite direction and repeat. Once or twice a year, wipe each slat with a cloth dampened with hot, soapy water. Dry thoroughly with a clean cloth—especially wooden blinds; otherwise they may warp.

Finessing Fabric Shades

Once a month, clean these using your vacuum's dust-brush tool. Dry clean them every year or so.

the CEILINGS

Dusting the Ceilings

No matter what your ceiling is made of, you're going to have to occasionally vacuum it to clear away the inevitable dust. Use the long brush attachment on your vacuum. If you choose to get up on a ladder and use a dust cloth instead, be mindful that this method will knock some debris onto the floor. While it is best to dust ceilings seasonally, a quick vacuum of obvious dust traps and spiderwebs can be easily incorporated into your vacuuming routine.

Scrubbing Acoustic Tile

Vacuuming will get off most dirt and dust, but you may need to give acoustic tiles a good scrubbing now and then. Use a mild all-purpose cleaning liquid and wipe down with a well-wrung sponge or cloth.

Picking Your Ceiling Paint

Most ceilings are painted with flat latex paint, which doesn't wash particularly well; water and detergent can leave streaks and spots. Eggshell, semigloss, high-gloss latex, and oil-based paints do wash well and can be scrubbed with a sponge. The kitchen ceiling will most likely need actual scrubbing due to grease buildup, but any ceiling is apt to get grimy from time to time. So if you see a spot, give it a blot.

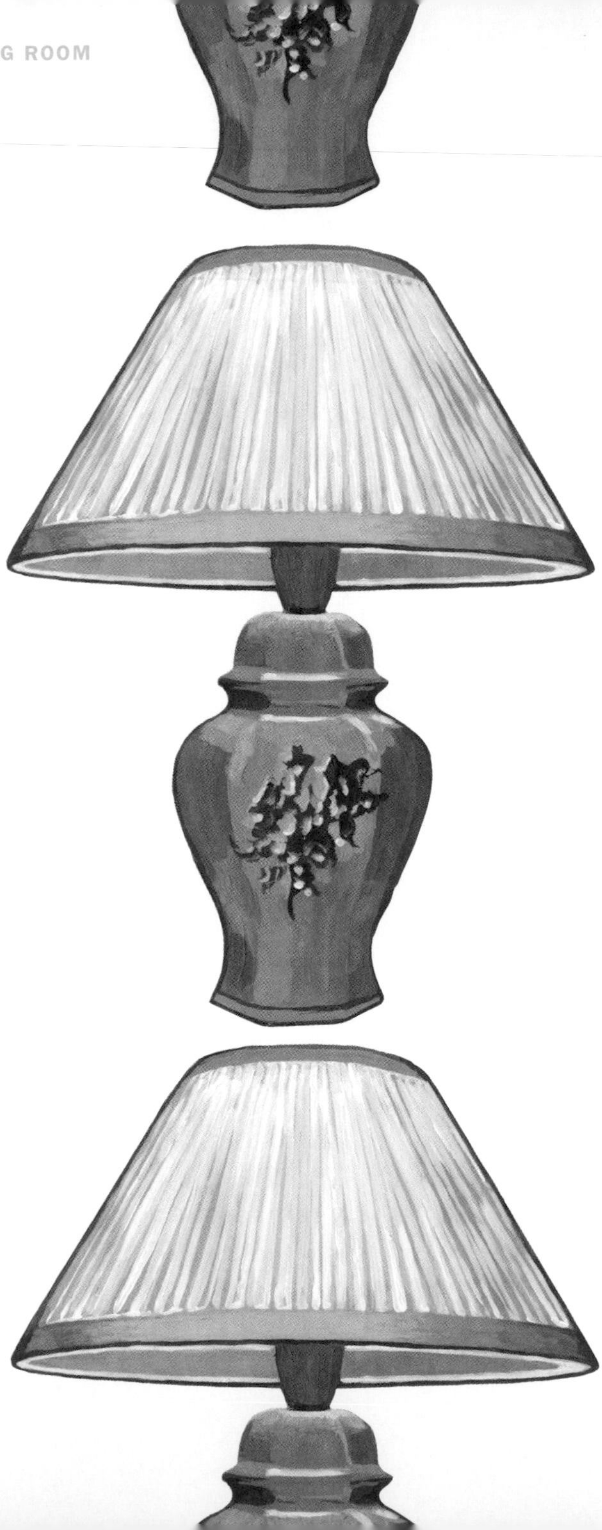

the LIGHT FIXTURES

Getting Light Fixtures to Shine

Before you do anything, unplug them—and this goes for any lamp or light fixture. For hanging lights, use an extendable duster to dust the hardware and cord. For wall sconces, remove the glass (if you can) about once a month and spray with glass cleaner. The best way to make chandelier crystals shine is to take them all off, if possible, and soak them in rubbing alcohol for about half an hour. (If you can't take them off, rub each one with rubbing alcohol and a clean cloth.) Dry each piece thoroughly. And don't take too long to put the pieces back, or you might forget where they go! Draw yourself a cheat sheet if you must.

Dusting Pleated Lamp Shades

I've found that the best way to get into these crevices is with a hand broom. Just sweep from the top of the shade to the bottom. I do this once every two weeks or so, since dirt builds up quickly.

Dusting Flat Shades

Using the smallest brush attachment, vacuum on the lowest setting, running the brush down the shade.

Washing Lamp Shades

If you notice obvious dirt and grime, use a cloth dampened with hot, soapy water to clean the shade. Don't use anything stronger than mild soap, however: Fabrics can discolor. If it's a valuable shade, take it to a professional.

WASTE NOT WANT NOT

My husband taught me to start replacing my regular incandescent bulbs with energy-efficient compact fluorescent lightbulbs (CFLs). Every time an old bulb burns out, I put in a CFL, which uses up to 75 percent less energy than a regular one and lasts for years. And the newest ones aren't glaring or harsh like you might think they'd be. They give off almost the same light. I say: Follow suit!

the ACCESSORIES

Cleaning Brass Candlesticks

Mix together equal parts white vinegar and salt and rub the candlesticks with a soft cloth.

Dusting Houseplants

Particularly if you have big-leafed plants, you'll need to wash each leaf to get the dust off. Hold the leaf in the palm of your hand so you don't damage it, and wipe it gently with a cloth barely dampened with water. (I'll admit it—this gets pretty boring after a while.) You can't do this with small-leafed plants, though. For those, fill a spray bottle with water, take the plants outside, and spray away.

Dealing with Brass or Copper Doorknobs

If you're lucky enough to have brass or copper doorknobs, make them shine! Add salt and flour in equal quantities to white vinegar until it turns into a paste, apply it to the knob, and buff to a high shine.

Cleaning Frames

I display my framed pictures on mantels, side tables, and bookshelves throughout the house. The frames are easy to clean: Just wipe the front of the glass with a piece of newspaper and a mixture of equal parts white vinegar and warm water. But spritz the paper, not the artwork, or moisture may seep into crevices. For more ornate frames with lots of nooks and crannies, blow them clean of dust and debris with a hairdryer using the cool setting.

my **HOUSE,** my **RULES**

Our bookshelf in the **FAMILY ROOM** is where I keep the knick-knacks that are most special to me. I have about twenty-two of them right now. One is a tea set from Japan that my mother got from her brother as a wedding present in 1931. What I do is **COLLECT THINGS** from the people in my life. As friends and family pass on, I go to their estates' auctions and try to buy items as **MEMENTOS**. I put a number on the bottom of each object, and I write the numbers in a book, along with where each item came from. This way, when my kids settle my stuff after I'm gone, they'll know **WHAT'S WHAT**.

FIXING UP the FIREPLACE

Having a fireplace is a joy, especially on cold Iowa nights. There's something about a fireplace with my family around it that just warms my heart. But with the pleasure comes responsibility. Take good care of your fireplace. Every fall, get a chimney sweep to make sure that your chimney isn't blocked and full of soot or birds' nests!

GAS or ELECTRIC

Wipe the glass or fiberglass door with a cloth dipped in an all-purpose cleaner, countertop spray, or window spray. You can also try white vinegar and newspaper for these, just as you would for cleaning other glass. Vacuum the interior with the brush attachment, then wipe it down with a damp rag afterward to get anything the vacuum may have missed. If you have a gas stove, it's a good idea to call in a pro to check for any gas leaks.

PELLET

Wood-pellet fuel is a fairly new thing, releasing no carbon dioxide into the environment. What will they think of next? A few cautions: If you leave the wood pellets in the hopper year after year, they can cause the unit to rust. So take them out after the heating season. Use a paintbrush to clean up all that debris, and vacuum the collection pan.

WOOD-BURNING

After each use, sweep out all those ashes and toss them into your compost pile if you have one. Clean the walls of the opening with a stiff brush, because that gunk can build up and catch on fire. Vacuum the screen with the brush attachment and wipe down glass doors with window spray or white vinegar and newspaper.

CLEANING
BRASS, CAST-IRON, or WROUGHT-IRON
SCREENS, ANDIRONS, and TOOLS

First, remove as much soot as you can with a damp cloth. Then dip a stiff brush in a mixture of warm water and laundry detergent, scrub the items thoroughly, rinse them with water, and dry them with a fresh cloth.

the ENTERTAINMENT

Battling the Boob Tube

Dust the screen with a damp cloth—and don't use the same cloth you used on anything else or you'll smear dirt all over. And make sure to vacuum the vents in the back using the brush attachment. We've always had a TV in the living room and just recently took one up to the family room. But I can't imagine anyone wanting to watch that one. It's not a very clear picture—you'd have to be pretty bored.

Disinfecting the Remote

Wipe down the tops and sides of all those buttons with a cotton ball slightly moistened with rubbing alcohol.

Sprucing Up the Speakers

Either spray with a can of compressed air or simply clean with a feather duster. If the cloth covering is detachable, take it off and rinse it in the sink with warm water. Let it dry thoroughly before replacing it, though.

Dusting Other Electronics

Wipe down all surfaces, paying attention to buttons and knobs, with a microfiber cloth. Spray any vents and the inside of the VCR/DVD cartridge door with a can of compressed air. (Don't use your vacuum here, as it can cause static electricity.)

Prettying Up the Piano

Clean a wooden piano as you would other wood furniture—with a cloth dampened with water and furniture polish. For ultra-glossy pianos, you don't want to use soap; it may dull that nice finish. Just rub the surface down with a piece of damp chamois. Dust the keys weekly with a clean paintbrush and occasionally wipe them with a damp cloth. If the keys seem dirty, wipe them with a cloth dampened with hot, soapy water, but make sure that it's dry enough that water doesn't run between the keys. If you have an antique piano, call in a professional: Don't try to rebuff ivory or wooden keys yourself.

ah, the MEMORIES

"I remember sitting around the living room ordering **BARBIE DOLLS** from the JC Penney catalog. When they arrived, Mom took one look at them and said, 'This is not reality! **GIRLS DON'T LOOK LIKE THIS**—they're going back!' So as quickly as those boxes had been opened they were closed back up and returned. Instead, we got **JANE WEST** dolls, plastic **PALOMINO PONIES**, and **FLAT-CHESTED** Tammy dolls."
— Monica (No. 3)

TV TIME in my house was **HIGHLY REGULATED.** I always knew what they were watching and when.

Or so I thought.

Sometimes they'd sneak in some TV time while I was taking a shower. You wonder, "How on earth do kids learn some of the things they do?" It's probably by **WATCHING TV.** One hot summer day when Dan was about three, he trotted into the living room with four bandages across his little nipple area. I asked, "What are you doing with all those **BANDAGES?**" He said, "IT'S SO THE MILK WON'T COME OUT."

CLEANING UPHOLSTERED
SOFAS, CHAIRS, and OTTOMANS

Every time I clean, I make it a point to vacuum my upholstery so that dirt and dust won't set in. And I always lift the cushions to suck up those cookie remnants and old peanuts. I also try to position the furniture so that it's out of direct sunlight to minimize fading. Here are some other tips:

LEATHER

Dust with a slightly damp microfiber cloth. Pull the furniture away from heating vents; hot air can dry leather out and cause it to crack.

COTTON AND LINEN

Most slipcovers can be machine-washed on the gentle setting; consult the label.

WOOL

This fabric requires dry-cleaning, but no more than once a year.

CHENILLE, CORDUROY, and VELVET

Use your vacuum's upholstery attachment, and be gentle so you don't cause the fabric to pill. These fabrics can be machine-washed in cold water and air-dried. Don't iron them, though—you may compress the fabric.

SILK

I've never bothered with fancy silk in my living room, but if you have it, take good care of it. Hand-wash silk slipcovers with mild detergent and let them air dry. Keep silk out of the sunniest spots; the sun is especially harsh on silk. If your piece of furniture is valuable, consider sending it out to be professionally cleaned.

CHECK THE TAGS

Generally, your furniture's tag or label will tell you the best way to care for it. Here's what those codes mean:

X

Vacuum only.

S

Spot-clean using a solvent cleaner only; water stains might become permanent.

S-W

Spot-clean with a solvent or water-based foam.

W

Spot-clean with mild detergent or upholstery shampoo.

REMOVING **STAINS** from **UPHOLSTERED FURNITURE**

As with laundry stains, the first thing you should do is remove any excess straightaway, and blot–don't wipe!–the spill with an absorbent cloth. Rinse the spot afterward with a damp sponge, and then dry it immediately. Fabrics differ, however, so test an inconspicuous spot before you treat. If your piece is valuable to you, don't hesitate to call in the professionals.

BEER	Dilute a teaspoon of mild detergent with a cup of lukewarm water and blot. Then mix up one part white vinegar with two parts water, and blot. Sponge it off.
BLOOD	First, blot with a cloth dampened in one teaspoon of mild detergent diluted in a cup of lukewarm water and blot. Still there? Dilute a tablespoon of white vinegar with a half-cup of water and blot. Sponge it off with clean water. Good as new!
BUTTER	Use a sponge dampened with dry-cleaning solvent and blot. Then blot with a cloth dampened with mild detergent and water.
CHOCOLATE	Dilute a teaspoon of mild detergent with a cup of lukewarm water and blot. Then mix one tablespoon of white vinegar with a half-cup of water and blot. Blot with the detergent mix again, and sponge it off with clean water. Repeat as necessary until the stain is gone.
INK	Dilute a teaspoon of mild detergent with a cup of lukewarm water and blot. Sponge it off.
JUICE and SOFT DRINKS	Blot with a cloth dampened in one teaspoon of mild detergent diluted in a cup of lukewarm water. Mix up one part white vinegar with two parts water, and blot, then sponge off with clean water.
WINE	Dilute a teaspoon of mild detergent in a cup of lukewarm water and blot. Then mix up one part white vinegar with two parts water, and blot, then sponge off.

CLEANING NON-UPHOLSTERED FURNITURE

Non-upholstered furniture is your best bet if you have kids or pets. Wood furniture especially stands the test of time. I think it looks even better with age, in fact. Shows its character.

ACRYLIC, LACQUER, and PAINTED WOOD

Pour one teaspoon of dishwashing liquid into a gallon of water. Apply to the furniture with a damp cloth.

ANTIQUE WOOD

Distilled water is great here, because it's extra gentle and won't harm a delicate finish. Dip a cloth in the water and wring it out—you don't want too much water on the wood. Dry immediately with a clean, soft cloth.

WOOD

Use your fingernail to get off any grime. Dampen a cloth with furniture polish and water and wipe the surfaces clean, then dry them thoroughly. Keep wood furniture out of direct sunlight so that it won't fade. And if you have a dining table with leaves, don't store the spare ones in a humid area, like a basement. Humidity may warp the wood.

WICKER

Use your vacuum's brush attachment to get at any loose dirt and crumbs stuck between the twigs; wipe the piece down with a mixture of cool water and a squirt or two of dishwashing liquid.

WAXING WOOD FURNITURE: It may seem like a fuss, but it actually keeps your furniture CLEANER by repelling DUST and SPILLS. Once every two months or so, after you've cleaned your wood furniture, apply an even layer of paste wax with a clean, soft cloth. Use an old TOOTHBRUSH to get into corners and crevices. Give the wax fifteen to thirty minutes to dry, then BUFF with a fresh cloth to remove all the wax.

PETS on the PREMISES

In general, I didn't let our dogs in the house, except for our last dog, Smoky—she was a little Chihuahua mix. Smoky was given to us by two little neighbor girls who lived across the street. Our girls were six, seven, and eight at the time; they just fell in love with Smoky, so I couldn't say no. The only problem with Smoky was that she wasn't house-trained. So she would wet the floor outside the upstairs bathroom door. That was her spot. But the kids adored her, so we kept her around for years and years anyway. If you have pets, here's how to clean up their living-room souvenirs:

TAKING PET HAIR OFF UPHOLSTERY Put on a pair of rubber gloves, pass your hands quickly under the faucet, and wipe down the upholstery in long strokes. And don't forget to tackle the source: Brush Fido and Fluffy regularly to remove any excess hair before it makes its way onto your favorite love seat.

REMOVING PET STAINS FROM UPHOLSTERY It's important to get to these as fast as you can, because that odor sure can linger. First, blot up as much as possible with a clean towel. Then mix a quarter cup of dishwashing liquid in a cup of water and use this to blot the spot again. Repeat. Last, apply an enzyme-based cleaner formulated to get out pet stains.

TRICKS of the TRADE
Mistakes happen. Here's how to fix them.

Getting a WATER RING off a WAXED WOOD TABLE

Here's one idea that occasionally does the trick: Combine four tablespoons of salt with three tablespoons of olive oil. Apply the solution to the spot and let it sit overnight. In the morning, wipe it off and wax the table. The real solution to this annoyance, however, is to teach kids (and guests!) to use coasters.

Removing WATER RINGS from UNTREATED WOOD FURNITURE

Your best bet for getting those stubborn rings out is sheer elbow grease. Rub at that stain with a soft cloth until you start to see results—it could mean half an hour! The cloth is gentle enough to do no damage and abrasive enough to get you results. No promises here, though: Sometimes a water ring is as permanent as they come.

Opening a PAINTED-SHUT WINDOW

Perhaps this doesn't come up too much anymore, but it's good to know nevertheless. Go along the whole edge of the window and try to knock it loose with the palm of your hand. You need to jar it a little bit. Or you can take a blunt tool like a putty knife, cover it with a cloth to protect the window, and use that to tap along the edge.

Taking GUM off CARPET

Put ice on the gum to freeze it, and scrape it off with a table knife. Ice always helps a sticky gum situation.

Getting TEA, FRUIT JUICE, or COLA DRINKS out of CARPET

Dip a cloth in a mixture of one cup warm water and one teaspoon mild detergent. Blot the stain. Then mix one-third of a cup white vinegar with two-thirds of a cup warm water and apply to the spot with a fresh cloth. Blot.

ANIMAL HOUSE

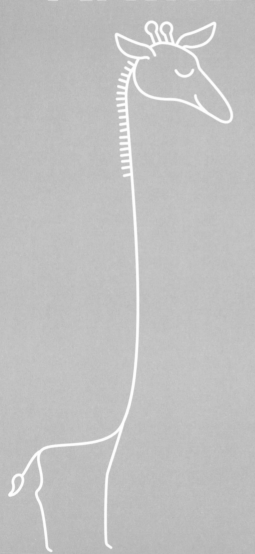

Vern worked as an engineer at John Deere, and every now and then we'd enjoy getting out of the house and attending one of his company's functions. One crisp fall night back in 1971, we went to a dance fund-raiser at the Val Air Ballroom in Des Moines. When we arrived at the dance, we were each handed a raffle ticket with a number on the back. I didn't even know what the raffle was for, but I said to Vern, "I really hope I win!" We had such a fantastic night, dancing to the jazz band and chatting with friends. I didn't even realize how many hours had passed until I heard someone say, "Now it's time for our much-anticipated, end-of-the-night raffle!" I frantically searched through my purse to find my ticket and pulled it out just in time to hear "Congratulations, number 103! Come up here and claim your prize!" I couldn't believe my eyes: I had ticket 103. "Vern, we won! We won!" I screamed, and ran right up onto the stage, full of excitement.

Until, that is, I saw what I had won: a person-sized papier-mâché giraffe. And it was painted all these crazy colors. I was just beside myself, but what was I to do? Everyone in the crowd was cheering for me and clapping like you wouldn't believe, so I graciously accepted my "prize" and walked off the stage in shock. It was getting to be time to go, so Vern grabbed the giraffe by the neck and hauled it through the parking lot to our maroon station wagon. We tried every which way to make it fit in the car. No luck. We finally just squeezed it in the best we could and kept the tailgate open. I was shivering the whole ride home as we drove down the highway with this big ole giraffe sticking out the back.

It was close to 1 a.m. by the time we pulled into the driveway. You should have seen us trying to take this thing out of the car. "Thelma, grab the legs," said Vern. "No, no, now just hold the tail so that it doesn't break." As we were shuffling around trying to get this monster through the front door I saw our neighbor Elsie stick her head out her bedroom window with a scowl on her face. "Don't you wish you had one of these?!" I called up to her. After we made our way through the front door, Vern asked, "Where the heck are we going to put this thing?" I said, "Let's take it upstairs to the family room for the time being." We got upstairs and propped up this giant animal in the corner of the room. I was amazed. I said to Vern, "It matches perfectly!" It worked like a charm in that room, that great big giraffe.

We were thrilled to climb into bed after such a long night, but morning came way too soon with a shriek from our youngest, Dan, who was five at the time. "There's a giraffe in the house! There's a giraffe in the house!" he kept screaming. So I ran out of the bedroom with my robe wrapped around me to find little Dan, in his light-blue firetruck pj's, frozen in the entryway of the family room like he'd caught Santa Claus in the act. Just couldn't believe his eyes. And I couldn't blame him. That giraffe was pretty impressive in the corner of our family room, right by the piano. It stayed with us for a good many years.

CHAPTER 4

a clean
BED
ROOM

I keep lots of things in my bedroom, from my favorite antique rocking chair to my jewelry to the dolls stashed in the closet, which I bring out when my grandchildren visit. And these aren't any ordinary dolls, mind you. Some are just plain ugly, and some are the silliest things I've ever seen. I have one that crawls really slowly and then falls over on its side out of nowhere and screams, "Momma! Momma! Momma!" But the one thing I don't have in my bedroom is a TV. I just don't believe in it. Bedrooms are for sleeping and getting dressed for parties and church and all that. Not for TVs. And not for kids. We have a lock on our bedroom door and always have. The only times the kids were let in was when one of them was sick. Even so, I'd inevitably hear the jiggling of the lock in the middle of the night, someone trying to sneak on in. We'd just ignore it, because that can get to be a real habit—kids coming in whenever they please, getting into bed with you. They have to learn to sleep on their own, bad dreams or not.

the FURNISHINGS 113

polishing WOOD DRESSERS, NIGHTSTANDS, and HEADBOARDS 113

lining DRESSER DRAWERS 113

cleaning PAINTED WOOD FURNITURE 113

cleaning UPHOLSTERY 113

dusting the LAMP SHADES, LIGHTBULBS, and TRACK LIGHTING 113

loosening a STUCK DRAWER 113

the FLOORS 114

VACUUMING the CARPET 114

washing HARDWOOD FLOORS 114

dusting the HEATING VENTS 114

the WALLS 114

tackling the DRAPES 114

getting CRAYON off the UPHOLSTERY 114

buffing up the venetian BLINDS 115

cleaning WALLPAPER 115

mastering ARTWORK 115

sprucing up SWITCH PLATES 115

the CEILING 116

conquering CEILINGS 116

cleaning the CEILING FAN 116

cleaning the CORNERS 116

dealing with DOOR FRAMES and MOLDINGS 117

the **BED** 117

getting UNDER the BED 117

VACUUMING the BED 117

FLIPPING the MATTRESS 117

AIRING OUT the MATTRESS 117

keeping PILLOWS FRESH 117

tackling MATTRESS STAINS 117

MAKING the BED 118

the **ACCESSORIES** 120

caring for BOOKS 120

dusting KNICKKNACKS 120

BEDROOM **STORAGE** 121

conquering the CLOSET 121

storing UNDERNEATH the BED 121

the **BABY'S** ROOM 122

cleaning the CRIB, CRADLE, and CHANGING STATION 122

getting FORMULA out of the carpet 122

keeping your **BEDROOM SPIC**-and-**SPAN** 123

making your **JEWELRY** SHIMMER and SHINE 124

TOOLBOX

BRUSHES
Paintbrush

BUCKETS, GLOVES, and MORE
Bucket or pail
Spray bottle

CLEANING PRODUCTS
All-purpose cleaning liquid
Baby wipes
Baking soda
Carpet cleaner
Dishwashing liquid
Mild detergent
Rubbing alcohol
White vinegar

CLOTHS, RAGS, SPONGES, and OTHER WIPERS
Brown paper
Chamois cloth
Cotton balls
Extendable duster
Microfiber cloth
Muslin
Old socks
Old T-shirt
Newspaper
Rag
Soft cloth

SWEEPING, MOPPING, and VACUUMING
Hand broom
Mop
Vacuum
with attachments

ODOR FIXERS
Chalk
Essential oil
Kitty litter
Lemon juice

STAIN REMOVAL
Iron
Upholstery shampoo

WAXING and POLISHING
Paste wax
Olive oil

HANDY to HAVE THESE AROUND
Can of compressed air
Hairdryer
Lint roller
Salt
Toothpaste
Vodka

the FURNISHINGS

Polishing Wood Dressers, Nightstands, and Headboards

For an earth-friendly way to make your furniture shine, whip up three parts olive oil to one part distilled white vinegar. Then put some nice clean socks on your hands, pour a bit of the mixture on them, and get to work. When you're all done, sprinkle some cornstarch on the surfaces and rub away; it'll soak up any excess oil and make your furniture shine up really glossy.

Lining Dresser Drawers

Lining your drawers will help keep your clothes fresher and the wood of your dresser cleaner. Instead of wasting money on special store-bought "liner paper," use leftover pieces of wallpaper or gift wrap—so much prettier too! If you're using wallpaper, just wet the edges of a trimmed piece and stick it inside the drawer. With gift wrap or any other paper you'd like to use, double-sided tape works well. And throw a sachet of lavender or pine in there while you're at it, for a lovely scent every time you open a drawer.

Cleaning Painted Wood Furniture

Squirt about a teaspoon of dishwashing liquid into a gallon of water. Wet your cloth, wring it out until it's damp, then wipe down your furniture.

Cleaning Upholstery

First, vacuum to get the bulk of the dust out. Then dampen a microfiber cloth and use it to wipe down the upholstery. It works great, and no cleaning products are needed. To care for specific types of upholstery, see page 100.

Dusting the Lamp Shades, Lightbulbs, and Track Lighting

Use your vacuum's brush or drapery attachment. Or go the even easier route and swipe lamp shades with a lint roller. If they're very dirty, you can usually take the shades off and give them a good soak in the bathtub with warm water and some dishwashing liquid. Dry them immediately with a hairdryer (set on low) so metal parts won't rust. And don't forget about that dusty bulb. Tackle it with a paintbrush. As for track lighting, use the vacuum's brush attachment. Or wrap an old T-shirt around a broom to get up there.

LOOSENING a STUCK DRAWER

Nothing's more frustrating than trying to open a dresser drawer that just won't budge. So rub a candle—or a bar of soap—on the top, bottom, and sides of the drawer. That will loosen it up in no time.

LIFE'S LITTLE ANNOYANCES

the FLOORS

Vacuuming the Carpet

Be sure to vacuum the carpet at least once a week, in long, overlapping strokes, paying close attention to the perimeter of the bed—this is where dust mites tend to gather. You'll need to treat thick rugs a little differently. I used to have a green shag carpet in the bedroom (it was just $5 a yard!), and it never showed dirt. And it was a wonder to walk on. But it was so thick that I'd have to use a rug rake to pull the long, matted fibers back and forth so that I could get the vacuum in there. So if you have a shag rug (they're back in style, you know—I almost regret getting rid of mine), adjust the height of the vacuum or the rug will wrap around the beater bar. And if you happen to move some furniture around and notice those pesky indentations in the carpet, place ice cubes in the spots; the moisture will help the carpet fluff right up.

Washing Hardwood Floors

Many people use white vinegar diluted in water, but that really won't do the job. Instead, use an all-purpose cleaner (diluted in water, per the instructions), and mop it around. Floors will get squeaky clean!

Dusting the Heating Vents

Vacuum vents with the brush attachment weekly to get dust out of them and allow the air to flow properly.

the WALLS

Tackling the Drapes

Whether you have cotton, linen, or wool drapes, take them outside about twice a year to air them out, or put them in the dryer on the air setting. If they're difficult to get off the rods, you can vacuum them with the drapery attachment on a low setting instead. Drapes shouldn't be washed more than once a year. When it's time, wash them in cold and hang dry. If you get a stain on them, first try a little bit of water. So many stains come out with just a little water. If that doesn't work, try carpet-stain remover.

GETTING CRAYON off the UPHOLSTERY

In addition to the walls (see page 92), kids will sometimes draw on furniture like beds, sofas, and chairs. Buy washable crayons if you want an easier life. If a stick figure appears on your favorite chair, get some brown paper (like a grocery bag) and place it on the crayon stain. Then iron right over the paper on a medium setting. The paper will absorb the crayon's oil. Remove what's left of the stain with an upholstery shampoo.

Buffing Up the Venetian Blinds

Here's a handy trick: Take them down and lay them in the tub with warm, soapy water for about a half hour. Use a cloth to get off any remaining dirt. Then hang them on the line to dry.

my HOUSE, my RULES

If your drapes have cords, take note: They can be very DANGEROUS in HOUSES WITH CHILDREN, so make sure the cords aren't where kids can get at them. Attach little METAL HOOKS to the walls to WRAP THE EXCESS cord around so that it doesn't hang.

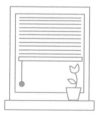

Cleaning Wallpaper

You can vacuum wallpaper with the brush attachment or gently clean the surface with a damp cloth dipped in dishwashing liquid. But be careful not to soak the paper or moisture may get into the seams and cause it to bubble up and pucker. You can also use a dry sponge (buy it at the hardware store); it will pick up dirt and dust from wallpaper like you wouldn't believe. Just use long strokes.

Mastering Artwork

Dust prints and paintings with a clean piece of muslin. If there's glass on the front, wipe it with a piece of newspaper and a mixture of equal parts white vinegar and warm water, but spritz the paper, not the artwork, or moisture may seep into crevices. For ornate frames with lots of nooks and crannies, blow them clean of dust and debris with a hairdryer using the cool setting.

Sprucing Up Switch Plates

Clean those grimy switch plates by wiping them with a cloth dampened with dishwashing liquid. If they're really nasty, you can remove them from the wall and soak them in warm, soapy water. If your plates are wrapped in wallpaper like mine are (Vern covers them so that everything matches), just vacuum them with the brush attachment.

the CEILING

Conquering Ceilings

Whenever you see something like a bug or a cobweb, get out the vacuum and the brush attachment and suck it up fast. If your attachment isn't long enough, look around the house for something to do the job, such as a fishing pole or a long broom or rake. Then cover the end with a rag or an old T-shirt and that'll work well, too.

Cleaning the Ceiling Fan

Take your shoes off, hop onto the bed, and wipe each blade with a wet rag—it needs to be wet so that you trap the dirt before it falls onto your pillow. If your ceiling fan isn't over the bed, use an extendable duster.

WASTE NOT WANT NOT

Don't be so quick to turn on the air conditioner; use a ceiling fan instead and you'll save lots of energy and money. It's got to be really hot in our house—80 degrees or so—before we'll use our air conditioner. I read recently that ceiling fans cost one cent an hour to run; air conditioners cost about fifty cents an hour. That's a big difference.

Cleaning the Corners

Corners can get really dusty. So use your vacuum's brush attachment to clean them every month or so, up high and down low.

ah, the MEMORIES

"Mom didn't have time to solve all of the **SQUABBLES** that arose among the nine of us, especially in the early days, when all four girls shared **ONE BEDROOM**. She let us work things out on our own unless it came to blows, or the screaming got to be too much. And it did, on more than one occasion. Sometimes we'd fight about the **CHORES**. But when Tim, Tom, and Monica went off to school, I was the oldest helper and 'got' to help mom **MAKE THE BEDS**. She told me that she could make a bed even with a person in it! Mom was a **NURSE**, and I remember thinking to myself, **WOW**. If that's what a nurse can do, then I **WANT TO BE A NURSE**."

— Maria (No. 4)

TACKLING MATTRESS STAINS

Apply a paste of baking soda and water to the spot with a soft cloth. Let it sit until dry, then brush the residue off with a hand broom or a clean cloth.

Dealing with Door Frames and Moldings

Dust tends to build up on these, so use an extendable duster or your vacuum's brush attachment.

the BED

Getting under the Bed

Don't forget this chore or else the dust that accumulates will eventually make the rug under the bed a different color from what's in the rest of the room. If your vacuum reaches all the way to the other side of the bed, great. Mine doesn't, so sometimes I'll have to lie on my belly to get everything clean under there. I also move the bed to a different area every so often.

Vacuuming the Bed

It's important to vacuum your mattresses frequently to get rid of dust mites, bacteria, and allergens. So every week, when you change your sheets, just vacuum the top.

Flipping the Mattress

At least twice a year, and four times if you've got the energy, you should flip your mattress to ensure even wear. Rotate it head to toe when you flip it, too.

Airing Out the Mattress

Every morning when you wake up, pull the sheets and blankets down toward the end of the bed to let it air out for an hour or so while you eat breakfast and get ready for the day. After a night of tossing and turning and what have you, it's the only civilized thing to do. Whenever you go away for a long period of time, take all the bedding off the mattresses and box springs to give them a breather, too. And once a year, it's important to give everything the full treatment: Strip your bedding and open the windows for a few hours. Mattresses typically last ten years; you'll know it's time to replace one if it's sagging in places.

Keeping Pillows Fresh

Pillows aren't the easiest things to wash, so cut down on your laundry time by placing them in zippered cases—many are treated to resist allergens—before putting them in pillowcases (the zippered side goes in first so it stays away from your pretty face). I label mine with a little masking tape and marker so that I can remember when I last washed them.

MAKING the BED

A well-made bed can instantly brighten a room in the morning and make you feel extra cozy tucked in at night. Making "hospital corners" is much easier than many people think—it's a lot like wrapping a present!

1 Spread the sheet out on the mattress and tuck in the bottom all the way across.

HOSPITAL CORNERS

2 Pull up one long side of the sheet and rest it on the bed. Tuck in the bottom part of this side—just like you'd fold in a corner of wrapping paper—and flop the rest of the sheet back over and tuck it in tightly under the mattress. Repeat for the other three corners.

3 Next comes the top sheet, and you can do hospital corners here too if you'd like. One little secret to a beautiful-looking bed is spreading the top sheet pattern-side down so that when you fold it over, the pattern can show its stuff—so simple, but it's one of those details that counts. Lay your blanket or quilt over the top sheet, grasp the top two corners of both the blanket and the sheet, and fold them back together.

4 If you use a fitted bottom sheet, just be sure to put enough muscle into it, stretching each corner of the sheet over its matching mattress corner nice and tight, so it won't curl up after a night of tossing and turning.

SMOOTH   FLUFF   RELAX

5 Be sure to smooth out any wrinkles! Fluff your comforter, throw it over the whole thing, and pile on the pillows.

If you treat your bed like the special place that it is, it'll thank you with a more restful sleep and a wonderfully peaceful feeling every time you enter your bedroom.

my **HOUSE,** my **RULES**

The kids just **LOVED TO READ**. Maria liked it so much that she'd go to the library to get her books and sit up in a tree so no one could **BOTHER HER**. The girls particularly liked *LITTLE WOMEN*, and the boys were always tickled with books about rocks. Tim liked mechanical things, so he was always READING ABOUT CARS; Tom loved books about sports; and Dan loved any books relating to **PLANES** or **TRUCKS**. (He'd draw pictures of trucks too.) When the kids were young, **I WOULD READ TO THEM** every day. One of their favorite things to have read to them was this little religious magazine for children called *MARYKNOLL*—it had big print, beautiful, colorful pictures, and when I read, I read with imagination and GUSTO—I think that's why our kids are the way they are now! So **OUTGOING** and **ANIMATED**.

the ACCESSORIES

Caring for Books

Take your books off the shelves and vacuum the spines and front and back covers with the brush attachment. And when you put them back, don't let them touch the wall. Leave about an inch between the books and the back of the shelf so that they can breathe and won't mildew. And keep them out of direct sunlight to minimize fading.

Dusting Knickknacks

Figurines, picture frames, and vases are dust magnets, you know. You can do one of two things: Dip ceramic or glass things in a tub filled with warm, soapy water and dry them with a clean towel, or dust them one by one with a damp cloth, a hairdryer, or your vacuum's brush attachment. You may need to stand on a stool to reach the ones that are up high. I know you're thinking no one sees the dust on those anyway, but if you don't dust them you'll take them down one day to find a three-inch layer of grime. So once every few months I'll stand on a stool and clean every single one of my collectibles.

BEDROOM **STORAGE**

Conquering the Closet

Clothes, shoes, and accessories tend to get musty over time. Every so often, open your closet doors and the windows to air everything out. Place a bowl of baking soda or kitty litter in there to absorb odors if it's really smelly. And whatever you do, don't go filling your closet with mothballs. They contain nasty chemicals. Put cedar blocks or lavender sachets inside instead. Or dip a cotton ball in an essential oil, such as geranium or rosemary, then tie it up in a hankie and hang it in the closet or place it in a drawer.

Storing underneath the Bed

If you live in an old house (or a tiny apartment in the city) with few closets, you should take advantage of the space beneath the bed. It's the perfect place to keep out-of-season clothing, extra linens, or sentimental hats you bought on that trip to Paris. Opt for canvas or cardboard boxes—they allow clothes to breathe, whereas plastic ones don't. You can also store clothes and linens in spare suitcases.

my **HOUSE,** my **RULES**

When the **KIDS WERE SMALL**, I'd pick out their outfits every single day. **NEVER** would I ask them what they wanted to wear. That was just asking for **TROUBLE**—and an argument! Kids look to their parents for the rules; when you ask what they want, you're telling them that you **DON'T HAVE CONTROL**, and that just makes them **NERVOUS**, even if they don't realize it.

THE BABY'S ROOM

Cleaning the Crib, Cradle, and Changing Station

Cribs, cradles, and changing stations are bound to get milk, formula, and much worse on them. So you just have to wash them down every week with hot water and a bit of mild soap. Don't use any harsh disinfectants in baby's room—I tend to believe that hot, soapy water does the trick and it does it without any unnecessary chemicals. You can use a bit of rubbing alcohol on stubborn spots. But never, ever use bleach around baby.

Getting Formula Out of the Carpet

These stains are the worst. Get to them quickly or live with them forever! As soon as you see a spot, dab it with a mixture of two cups of warm water and one tablespoon of dishwashing liquid. Keep blotting until the spot's gone.

my **HOUSE,** my **RULES**

I remember the only **ROCKING CRADLE** we had was one that Vern made for me out of **PINE**. Not **FANCY**, mind you, it was very plain, but it worked— **WORKED LIKE A CHARM**. It had a string on it so that I could lie in bed and **PULL THE STRING** to rock the baby a little bit until he or she went to sleep.

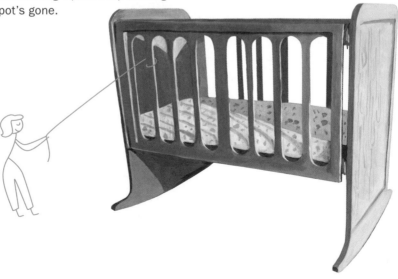

KEEPING YOUR BEDROOM
SPIC-and-SPAN

If you have guests on their way over, your first priority probably isn't straightening up the bedrooms. But generally, keeping your bedrooms dusted and clean is the best thing that you can do for yourself and your family. A cozy and clean bedroom is not just a pleasure—it's a necessity!

DAILY

Open the windows when you get up. Throw the bed covers back—a little air in there will help to clear that sleepy bed smell. If you can keep the windows open all day, I say do it. The fresher it stays in your bedroom, the better you'll sleep. Make the bed and fluff the pillows. Hang up robes and nightgowns near a window to air them out. Tidy up any messes.

WEEKLY

Change those sheets! Bodies are full of natural oils and perspiration. Change them more frequently if someone has been sick. Sheets go right against your skin, so I tend to favor cotton, cotton blends, flannel, or synthetics—you can wash any of these in hot water to kill the bacteria. I don't much care for fancy silk sheets that require cold water washing or, worse yet, dry-cleaning. Dust the bedroom thoroughly and vacuum the floors, draperies, and shades.

ONCE or TWICE A YEAR

Wash pillows and comforters. Turn the mattress and flip it. Launder the mattress covers, pads, blankets, and comforter covers.

MAKING YOUR JEWELRY SHIMMER and SHINE

Time can tarnish a perfectly lovely bauble.
Here's how to get your gems to sparkle.

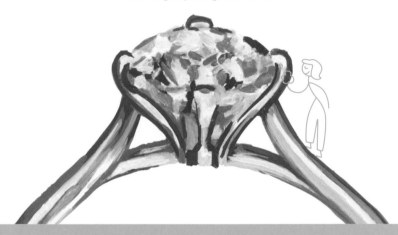

GOLD AND PLATINUM Soak gold and platinum pieces in equal parts warm water and rubbing alcohol; rinse and lay on a towel to dry.

PEARLS Dip a soft cloth in warm water and a touch of mild detergent; gently clean each pearl (whether it's part of a necklace, bracelet, or earrings) and lay flat on a towel to dry. Store in a velvet cloth rather than plastic, which can cause pearls to dry out.

STERLING SILVER Rub toothpaste onto your jewelry and rub it off with a soft cloth. To store, wrap in acid-free paper and place in a plastic bag.

DIAMONDS Pour some vodka in a bowl and place your diamond pieces inside; let sit for a few minutes, rub with a soft toothbrush, and rinse with water. Lay on a towel to dry.

COSTUME JEWELRY Put a piece of chalk in your jewelry box so that pieces won't tarnish.

If you're having TROUBLE SLEEPING—the day's events may be running amok in your head, or your dInner might not be sitting quite right—try putting a fresh pillowcase on your pillow. Sometimes the clean, cool feeling against your skin can calm you down and put you right to sleep!

a FALL from
GRACE

When I was a young girl, I won a ceramic statue of the Blessed Mary at the St. Augustine church bazaar, which took place in Fidelity, Kansas, just south of Sabetha. The statue stood about a foot and a half high, and I kept it atop my dresser. When I married Vern, the Blessed Mary came with me, and I displayed her on the dresser in our bedroom in Granger.

That tall dresser is also where I kept one of my other favorite things: my chocolates. I believe firmly that good chocolate is good for you, in moderation, of course. But kids don't need sweets lying around within arm's reach, so I kept my chocolates in my off-limits-to-the-kids bedroom. One lazy summer day, Maria and I were about to take a walk around the neighborhood. I looked outside and the sun was glaring bright, so I went into the bedroom to grab my hat, and told four-year-old Maria—whom I had carefully dressed in her pink flowered dress—to stand right in the doorway to wait for me. "Don't move, Maria. You know the rules: No kids allowed in the bedroom!" "Okay, Mommy," she said.

I headed for the closet to grab my hat. And just when I had it in my hand—BANG! It was one of those really scary bangs, where you're afraid to see what happened. There was Maria, on the floor, surrounded by four of my whitewashed dresser drawers. My clothes and jewelry were all strewn about, not to mention my unmentionables. She had pulled out the bottom drawer to step on it and get to the top of the dresser, and the whole thing just toppled over on her. She was trying to get to my chocolates, which she'd spotted from the doorway. Thankfully, she wasn't hurt. Such a brave little thing—she didn't even cry. But my Blessed Mother didn't fare as well. Her body just broke right off during the fall. Luckily, Vern is pretty handy. He sawed off the broken edges and reinvented my Blessed Mother as a bust, which sits on top of my dresser to this day. I sure learned my lesson: No kids in the bedroom, but if you must let them in, hide the candy.

CHAPTER 5

a clean HOME OFFICE

Our home office wasn't always a home office. It used to be Tom and Tim's room—Vern built two twin beds end to end, complete with drawers underneath. (At one time, I walked around the house and counted fifty-four drawers that Vern had built.) The room had paneled walls and black-and-white tile floors.

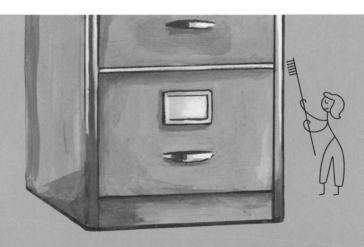

But in 1985, when our last child left the nest, we decided to turn that upstairs bedroom into something we could use for ourselves. Vern tore out the built-in twin beds and replaced them with an off-white Formica desktop, with a four-drawer cabinet on the left and two steel file cabinets on the right. (As you can see, I married a very handy man. Women often approach me, saying "Aren't you lucky. I wish I could get my husband to hammer a nail.") We put in new carpet and filled the grooves in the paneled walls so that I could wallpaper the room to match the Formica.

In one corner we have an exercise bike, though we don't use it often. Most exercise is done walking the stairs two or three times a day to check e-mail. We have a sleeper sofa in there, too—it's great for a quick nap or for when the grandchildren visit. The bookshelves are filled with Vern's toy John Deere tractors, which the children have given him over the years. The shelves also feature Vern's genealogy books. For twenty-five years, he's researched his and my families through a total of nine generations. At first I had reservations about this research, because I didn't know any of these dead people. But I've very much enjoyed meeting the living relatives in Europe and all over the United States.

We set the room up so that there's plenty of space for our computer, printer, scanner, TV, radio, and phone. Having a dedicated home office is a great way to keep up with modern technology—to access information quickly and share our lives with family. A home office is also an essential space for getting things done, especially if you have a busy household like we always did. Having this room, and keeping it clean and organized so you can get to the important stuff, is an absolute necessity.

the **COMPUTER** 133

cleaning the COMPUTER 133

tackling the TOWER 133

making the MONITOR SHINE 133

cleaning the KEYBOARD 133

perfecting the PRINTER 134

getting the MOUSE SQUEAKY CLEAN 134

cleaning a LAPTOP 134

the **DESKS**, **CABINETS**, and **BOOKSHELVES** 134

cleaning out the DESK 134

keeping GADGETS DUST-FREE 134

sprucing up the SHELVES and FILE CABINETS 134

dusting BOOKS 135

maximizing VERTICAL SPACE 135

KEEPING LIKE THINGS TOGETHER 135

keeping the **HOME OFFICE** under **CONTROL** 136

preventing PAPER-SHREDDER JAMS 136

putting PAPER in its PLACE 136

conquering CORDS 136

the **PHONE** 138

cleaning the CORD 138

disinfecting the RECEIVER AND BASE 138

getting a CORDLESS PHONE to CHARGE 138

RECYCLING YOUR **ELECTRONICS** 139

INK-JET CARTRIDGES 139

FLOPPY DISKS 139

CELL PHONES 139

COMPUTERS 139

MANAGING YOUR **HOUSEHOLD** 140

HOLDING on to **MEMORIES** 142

making a SCRAPBOOK 143

TOOLBOX

BRUSHES
Paintbrush

CLEANING PRODUCTS
Dishwashing liquid
Rubbing alcohol
Window-cleaning liquid

**CLOTHS, RAGS, SPONGES,
and OTHER WIPERS**
Cloth
Cotton swabs
Microfiber cloth
Rag

**SWEEPING, MOPPING, and
VACUUMING**
Broom
Mop
Vacuum
with attachments

**HANDY to HAVE
THESE AROUND**
Can of compressed air
Cornstarch

the COMPUTER

Cleaning the Computer

Before you do anything, turn it off (this goes for all of your electronics, by the way). Use a microfiber cloth to tackle dust—a paintbrush can work, too.

Tackling the Tower

Wipe the exterior with dishwashing liquid and water. It's best to place the tower on a hard surface, like a wood floor or a piece of plywood, while you clean; carpet fibers can get into the system and clog it up.

Making the Monitor Shine

For standard CRT (cathode-ray tube) screens, dampen a microfiber cloth with window-cleaning liquid and some water and wipe away. For fancier LCD or plasma screens, barely dampen a lint-free cloth. Don't use a microfiber cloth because it may scratch the screen. And never spray anything onto the screen; moisture can seep in and cause damage.

WASTE NOT WANT NOT

Instead of tossing your used dryer sheets, use them to wipe the computer monitor free of dust. They're great for taking away the static electricity that tends to attract dust in the first place.

my HOUSE, my RULES

I make sure that all of my **IMPORTANT** stuff stays together in a binder so that **IF I NEED** something, I can access it easily. I keep our **MARRIAGE** certificate, the kids' **BIRTH** certificates, the **DEED** to our house, our insurance policies, and our wills in a locked and fireproof place in the home office. I also keep a copy of everything in the **SAFE DEPOSIT BOX** at the bank, just in case!

Cleaning the Keyboard

Turn it upside down and shake it gently over a wastepaper basket to get out those cookie crumbs. Then use a can of compressed air to blow dust and dirt off; use short bursts of air rather than long ones or condensation may form. If you spilled something on the keyboard and there's a sticky, gooey mess, try taking off a few keys and cleaning beneath them with a damp cloth. If the keys still aren't working right, take a trip to the repair shop.

Perfecting the Printer

Dip a cloth in rubbing alcohol and wipe down the exterior, including all the buttons. Check your manual for instructions on cleaning the interior. Keep e-mail printing to a minimum to save paper, and reuse both sides of the paper when you can. It's as simple as that.

Getting the Mouse Squeaky Clean

Flip the mouse over and twist off the disk on the bottom that holds the ball. Pop the ball into your hand and clean it with a cloth dampened in a mixture of dishwashing liquid and water. Then clean the area where the ball goes and wipe down the exterior.

Cleaning a Laptop

Use a can of compressed air to get dust off the keyboard. Wipe down the exterior with a cloth dampened in dishwashing liquid and water.

the DESKS, CABINETS, and BOOKSHELVES

Cleaning Out the Desk

Every few months or so, take all that junk out of your desk drawers and weed through it, shredding papers you no longer need, recycling anything recyclable, and tossing any trash. Then use your vacuum's brush attachment to clean the insides of the drawers before wiping them down with dishwashing liquid and water. As for the top of the desk, most materials (glass, wood) can be cleaned by wiping them with a bit of soapy water.

Keeping Gadgets Dust-Free

Whenever you go on vacation, unplug your electronics and cover them with plastic bags to keep dust out.

Sprucing Up the Shelves and File Cabinets

Take everything off the shelves and vacuum or dust. Wipe down the shelves with a rag dampened with warm, soapy water; let them dry thoroughly before putting everything back.

Dusting Books

Use a microfiber cloth (no soap needed) to dust books, whether they have cloth covers or hard plastic ones. And books don't do well with sunlight; it fades them fast. So whenever possible, keep them out of direct light.

Maximizing Vertical Space

Most home offices aren't huge; they may be tucked into a corner of the kitchen or carved out from a section of a guest bedroom. So use all available space to your advantage. Place stackable bins on or under the desk. Store file cabinets in your closet, if you have one nearby. Consider stackable bookcases, too. Hang file-folder holders, corkboards, and magnetic boards on the walls. Or paint one wall in chalkboard paint, so that you can write yourself to-do lists and feel like a kid playing on the sidewalk.

Keeping Like Things Together

The worst is when you sit down to pay a bill and have to look in three different drawers to find your stamps, envelopes, and calculator. So invest in drawer organizers, and keep all of your bill-paying stuff in one section and your personal stationery and nice pens in another.

WASTE NOT WANT NOT

If you have a box of electronic equipment lying around in the closet, the worst thing is for moisture to get inside and ruin all the components. Grab an old pair of pantyhose, cut off a leg, fill it with kitty litter, and tie a knot at the top. Put it in the box to absorb excess moisture.

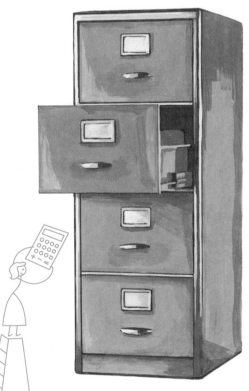

KEEPING the HOME OFFICE UNDER CONTROL

Home offices, I find, can go from calm to chaotic in a jiffy. It helps to know how to curb clutter and keep everything running smoothly and neatly.

PREVENTING PAPER-SHREDDER JAMS

Once in a while it's a good idea to lubricate the blades with shredder oil so the machine will continue to run smoothly. Consult your manual for the specific kind of oil to use with your shredder. Squirt the oil in a line onto the blades through the paper opening; run the machine in reverse for ten to twenty seconds to help distribute the oil evenly. Then feed a few pieces of paper through to remove any residue.

PUTTING PAPER IN ITS PLACE

To stop that junk mail and endless array of unsolicited catalogs from invading your life, go to the Federal Trade Commission's website (www.ftc.gov) and type "unsolicited mail" into the search area. You can actually block your address and cut down on this kind of clutter. Also, remember to always check the "opt out" box whenever you purchase anything online or fill out a new credit card application. Junk mail is a silly waste.

CONQUERING CORDS

Use heavy-duty tape to affix excess cords to the underside of your desk instead of having a heap of them on the floor. Or drill a hole cut in the back of your desk to help keep the cords out of sight. Stash your spare cords in a labeled, resealable bag; otherwise, months from now you won't know which gadgets they belong to.

Make your home office a KID-FREE zone!
When my grandchildren Cale and David snuck into Vern's office and messed with his computer, he surprised them the next day by hooking all the gadgets up to a **HIDDEN CONTROL SWITCH**. If he decides to flip the switch, no one is getting on that computer. Not even me! Makes me long for the days of the plain old **TYPEWRITER**.

the PHONE

Cleaning the Cord

Take the cord off the phone and rub it with a mixture of water and dishwashing liquid. Dry it completely with a separate cloth before reattaching it to the phone.

Disinfecting the Receiver and Base

You wouldn't believe all the germs and grime that build up on your phone receiver and buttons. Use dishwashing liquid and water to wipe down the phone. Dampen cotton swabs in rubbing alcohol to clean up between the buttons.

Getting a Cordless Phone to Charge

Sometimes it seems like your cordless phone just won't charge. If that's the case, rub those metal parts on the base with a pencil eraser. Now try again.

my HOUSE, my RULES

Nowadays, people have more than one line, **CALL WAITING**, and caller ID. Well, we had one phone line and some pretty **STRICT RULES** about it. Nobody needs to be on the phone all day. Do your business or make your plans, then **WRAP IT UP.**

RECYCLING YOUR ELECTRONICS

Gadgets get updated so quickly these days that it's easy to all of a sudden be left with an obsolete gizmo. And who wants to be behind the times? But many of these devices have parts that can be reused, which is a good thing since tossing these items in the trash wreaks havoc on the environment. Your local electronics shop may have a recycling box where you can drop your castoffs. Here are some additional guidelines:

INK-JET CARTRIDGES	Don't toss these into the trash; they're not biodegradable. Instead, you can drop HP, Lexmark, or Dell ink-jet cartridges off at your local Staples and get $3 in Staples Rewards (it's a free program) for each one. Just keep in mind that you're limited to bringing in three cartridges at a time. When you buy a new cartridge, see if it came with a prepaid envelope for returning the used one (many do).
FLOPPY DISKS	Still got these lying around? Visit WWW.EARTH911.COM to find drop-off locations in your area.
CELL PHONES	Some cell phone companies accept all brands of cell phones for recycling. Visit WWW.RACETORECYCLE.COM/CONSUMER.HTML, where you can print a free-postage label. You might also investigate various places to donate your phone. Whether you'd like to give to the military or to a women's shelter, your phone donations will likely be warmly accepted. You can also drop off old cell phones at many electronics stores.
COMPUTERS	Many companies take back computers for recycling. Check out WWW.MYGREENELECTRONICS.ORG/RECYCLECORPPROGRAMS.ASPX for listings.

MANAGING
YOUR HOUSEHOLD

I just can't stand clutter. Since running a family of eleven required a lot of paperwork, I had to stay on top of everything or papers would just pile up. It helps to have a good system.

Keep paper piles at bay by taking time each week to go through your receipts and record them, then shred (or file away) the actual receipts. Prevent coupon craziness by going through your stack regularly and throwing out those that have expired.

Create a file for each member of your family to hold passports, birth certificates, social security cards, and other valuable documents. Consider placing the originals in a safe deposit box and keeping the copies at home.

Get yourself an accordion folder. They are lifesavers. File the year's papers—from bills and cancelled checks to expenses—alphabetically. At the end of the year, go through the file and move only the papers you need to keep (see chart at right) into permanent file drawers or boxes. Shred the rest.

ALWAYS KEEP

birth, marriage, and death certificates

adoption and custody papers

citizenship and naturalization papers

separation and divorce papers

settlement agreements

military documents

social security cards

diplomas and school transcripts

medical histories

employment records

audit records

insurance records

IRA contribution records

tax returns and supporting documentation

passports

KEEP WHILE ACTIVE

motor vehicle titles, purchase receipts, and licenses

records of auto service and repair

copies of auto insurance cards and registrations

KEEP 7 YEARS

stocks, bonds, and other securities

bank accounts, account of ownership registers, and statements

list of credit, ATM, and debit cards, credit contracts, records of credit payments, and account statements

receipts and records of deductible expenses, income, and tax payments

HOLDING on to MEMORIES

There are so many things you can do to keep the past alive. For the last few years, Vern's been working on his family tree in our home office. I like to put together collections of photographs. Everybody may have digital cameras these days, but my old photos from when the kids were growing up—and even from when I was growing up—are so precious, and keeping them clean and beautiful for years to come is important to me. My photos are organized in albums and scrapbooks. I am creating a special photo album for each of my kids' fiftieth birthdays. Four down, five more to go!

MAKING a SCRAPBOOK

1 Buy a blank book filled with acid-free paper. Steer clear of albums with sticky pages. That glue will eat away at your photos over time and leave you with a sad mess.

2 Instead, use adhesive corner mounts to secure your photos to each page—you can even make your own out of ribbon, scraps of wrapping paper, or any sturdy paper you have lying around. It's simple: Cut some 1½-by-¾-inch pieces. Fold down the top two corners of one of the long sides to make a triangle—like you're making a paper airplane. Stick a piece of tape along the seam to hold it together (or if you're using ribbon, iron the triangle flat), and repeat for the other three corners. Tuck your photo into all four corners with the seamless side up, put a bit of double-sided tape or glue on the back of the corners (making sure not to get any on the photo), and place it into the book. Not only will your photos stay put, they'll be beautifully accented with your very own handiwork.

FOLDING PHOTO CORNERS

3 When you've filled up a book—or when you just need a break and want to put it away for a while—make sure to store it in a safe, dry place, away from heaters, damp objects, and little grubby hands. If your photos get dusty or oily, just use a dry cotton ball to gently rub away the dirt and debris!

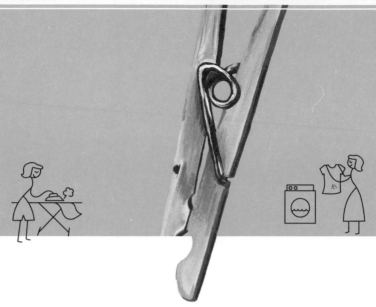

CHAPTER 6

clean LAUNDRY

I like doing laundry. I really do. But with nine kids, I used to have to do the laundry every day. And multiple times during the day! So I tried to cut corners wherever I could. There were days when one of the kids would bring down some pants or pajamas and I'd say, "Well, this looks perfectly clean!" I'd look at it, smell it, think that it smelled fine to me, fold it back up, and put it in their pile. They never knew it wasn't washed. If it didn't smell, it didn't get washed. That was my rule. Because it saved me time, it saved water and energy, and it saved the garment too. The more you wash something, the faster it's going to wear out.

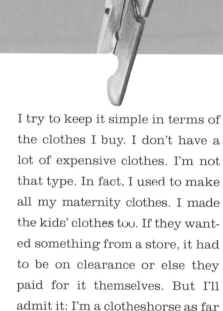

Part of the reason I enjoy doing the laundry so much is the great laundry room that Vern fixed up for me. The pantry closet has a long slot to hold the ironing board. I have a retractable clothesline for hanging my unmentionables and even my plastic bags after I wash them out. And I have two utility sinks that come in handy for just about everything. Like hand-washing my hose.

I try to keep it simple in terms of the clothes I buy. I don't have a lot of expensive clothes. I'm not that type. In fact, I used to make all my maternity clothes. I made the kids' clothes too. If they wanted something from a store, it had to be on clearance or else they paid for it themselves. But I'll admit it: I'm a clotheshorse as far as the clearance rack goes. I do love a clearance rack.

giving **CLOTHES** some **TLC** 149

SWEATERS 150

COTTON **BUTTON-DOWN** SHIRTS 151

DRESS **PANTS** 151

JEANS 151

SOCKS 153

T-SHIRTS and COTTON **DRESSES** 153

SWEATPANTS and **SWEATSHIRTS** 153

WORKOUT WEAR 153

tending to **OUTERWEAR** and **ACCESSORIES** 153

DOWN-FILLED JACKETS 153

FLEECE PULLOVERS 153

HATS, **GLOVES**, and **SCARVES** 153

LEATHER **HANDBAGS, BELTS**, and SHOES 154

GETTING FANCY about **FOOTWEAR** 154

SNEAKERS 154

SLIPPERS 154

FLIP-FLOPS 154

treating **TEXTILES** 155

SHEETS and PILLOWCASES 155

washing **BLANKETS** AND **PILLOWS** 155

DRYING BLANKETS and **COMFORTERS** 155

QUILTS 156

MATTRESS PADS 156

SHOWER CURTAINS 156

TOWELS 157

RUGS 157
CURTAINS 157
TABLECLOTHS and NAPKINS 157

dealing with DELICATES 158
FINE BRAS and LINGERIE 158
EVERYDAY BRAS and LINGERIE 158
UNDERWEAR 158
PANTYHOSE 158
SWIMSUITS 158

washing BABY CLOTHES 160

getting IRONING STRAIGHT 162
IRONING CLOTHING and LINENS 164
BUTTON-DOWN SHIRTS 164
PANTS 164
SILK TIES 164
TABLECLOTHS 164

maintaining the LAUNDRY ROOM 165
emptying the DRYER'S LINT TRAP 165
cleaning the DRYER'S VENT 165
sanitizing the WASHER 165
tackling the WASHER'S and DRYER'S EXTERIORS 165
cleaning a STICKY IRON 165

translating CLOTHING LABELS 166

tackling STAINS in a FLASH 168

TOOLBOX

BRUSHES
Horsehair

BUCKETS, GLOVES, and MORE
Spray bottle

CLEANING PRODUCTS
All-purpose cleaning liquid

Baking soda

Borax

Club soda

Dishwashing liquid

Hydrogen peroxide

Mild detergent

Rubbing alcohol

Shampoo

White vinegar

CLOTHS, RAGS, SPONGES, and OTHER WIPERS
Paper towel

Rag

SWEEPING, MOPPING, and VACUUMING
Broom

Mop

Vacuum
with attachments

ODOR FIXERS
Lemon

STAIN REMOVAL and LAUNDRY SUPPLIES
Baby detergent

Clean towel

Clotheslines

Delicate wash

Dryer sheets

Enzyme presoak

Golf balls

Iron

Mild detergent

Oxygen bleach

Pretreatment product

Stain remover

Talcum powder

Turkish towels

Zippered mesh bags

WAXING AND POLISHING
Shoe cream

Wax polish

HANDY to HAVE THESE AROUND
Clean white socks

Cornmeal

Eyedropper

Lemon juice

Salt

Plastic spatula

Towel

Washing soda (or sodium carbonate)

GIVING CLOTHES
SOME TLC

Before we get started, here are a few important things you should know. My "golden rules," if you will.

Some people just throw their whites in with their colors without thinking too much about it. I'm here to tell you from experience: Do not do this! One time I washed something red in my whites by accident, and you can guess what happened. Yup, pink clothes all around. Always sort, or you risk ruining your clothes and wasting money to boot. So we're clear, I rarely wear things like silk that require dry-cleaning. So if you have something you truly, truly love, whether it's an heirloom quilt or a one-of-a-kind sweater, you might just want to leave it to the professionals. Take good care of the things that give you delight.

You're going to notice I don't suggest tossing too many things in the dryer. Dryers use a great deal of energy, which means big electricity bills. Hanging laundry to dry not only saves you money, it saves your clothes too: No shrinkage! If you don't have outdoor space, I recommend investing in a standing drying rack.

There are a couple of ways to machine-dry that won't cost you an arm and a leg: Become best friends with the air-fluff and spin-dry settings. Say you have a special coat or a nice quilt that smells musty, but you don't want to put heat on it. Toss it in the dryer and use the air-fluff setting to freshen it up and get the wrinkles out—no harm done.

As for spinning dry: After hand washing your hose, bras, and delicate sweaters, place them in the washer and turn on the spin cycle to get rid of the excess water. The clothes will dry faster than if you'd just hung them on the line right away. For years I used to roll everything in a towel, and then I'd have this sopping wet towel lying around. Not anymore.

my **HOUSE,** my **RULES**

Keeping your clothes **CLEAN, PRESSED,** and **NICE** isn't vanity, it's an essential way to **FEEL GOOD** about yourself. Wearing **MESSY CLOTHES** isn't how I want to present myself to the world, and I taught my kids to **TAKE PRIDE** in their appearance, too.

Sweaters

To make sure they keep their shape and don't stretch out, hand-wash knits in cold water with mild detergent. Gently squeeze out the water (no wringing!), put them in the washer on the spin cycle to get out any remaining water, and machine-dry them for just a minute to minimize those pesky wrinkles. Pat them into shape and lay them flat on the ironing board to dry. Okay, I'll admit it: I just shrunk a sweater because I didn't realize it was wool. I put it in the dryer, then pulled it out and it was half its original size. Whoops! So just be careful and read those labels. Because a lot of fabrics today look alike, and you need to make sure you know what you're dealing with.

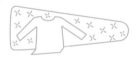

WASTE NOT WANT NOT

I'm a very frugal user of soap, and you should be, too. The truth is, you just don't need a lot—and too much can actually dull bright fabrics or leave a residue. So don't think that using more than the directions indicate will get your clothes or linens any cleaner.

my **HOUSE,** my **RULES**

It's never a good idea to store clothing in **PLASTIC**. You know how you get stuff back from the dry cleaner in those plastic bags? Don't keep them around, because plastic doesn't allow fabrics to **BREATHE**. Instead, wrap your seasonal clothing in old pillowcases or sheets. And speaking of **STORAGE**, I don't know about your closets, but mine can't store big, **BULKY THINGS**. Do as I do: Store clothing in a **CEDAR CHEST** to keep out moths. Line it with unbleached and undyed muslin (find it at fabric stores) so that your clothes don't come in contact with the wood; that could deteriorate fabrics over time. I store my favorite things in that chest, including the **WHITE TAM** I bought on my recent trip to Paris with all my girls. I bought them tams too, but no one wore them except me.

Cotton Button-Down Shirts

Unroll the sleeves and unbutton the buttons before tossing shirts in the wash or your buttonholes may tear during the cycle. Wash them in cold water, then machine-dry them for just a few minutes before hanging them on the line.

Dress Pants

Don't forget to empty your pockets of coins, pens, and tissues. I've learned this the hard way, after washing one of Vern's shirts only to see a pen floating on top of the water one time too many. Wash dress pants separately from other clothes and in cold water. Air-fluff them, then hang on the line and press them when they're slightly damp—it gets out all the wrinkles.

Jeans

Make sure you sort like with like—light jeans with other light jeans, dark ones with dark. Otherwise dyes may run and ruin the whole lot. Turn jeans inside out to prevent fading and those white soap-residue streaks. And try to clean jeans in small loads to cut down on abrasion. Wash them in cold water, then stretch the waistbands and legs a bit (because jeans tend to shrink). Machine-dry them for just a few minutes to get those wrinkles out; if you dry them until they're bone dry you may damage the fibers. Press them when damp to get the crease right. Hang to dry.

ah, the MEMORIES

"Monday morning was the primary day for **LAUNDRY**. Though Mom was the one who did the laundry, it was **OUR RESPONSIBILITY** to get it all downstairs and then hang it out on the line when she was done, because she wasn't big on **DRYERS**. But doing the laundry didn't mean just tossing the clothes in and that was that. Oh, no. Mom **RECYCLED THE WATER**. Let me explain: She would start with the cleanest clothes, usually the whites, and then **STOP THE WASHER** before the water drained. She'd then put the washed clothes in a rubber tub, using a wooden spoon to transfer them if the water was too hot. Then she'd drop the next load in, using that same water, **RUN THE WASH CYCLE**, and REPEAT THE PROCESS two to three times, depending on how dirty the water was. She'd toss all the clothes back in and run the rinse cycle. My guess is that she did **TWELVE TO FIFTEEN LOADS** on Mondays and then another THREE TO SIX every other day of the week." — Jane (No. 6)

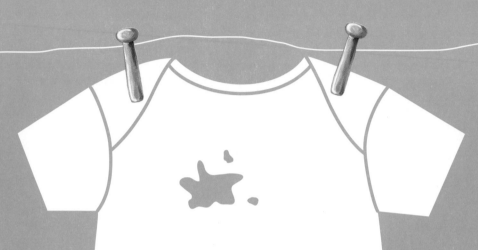

Keep a bottle of stain remover in your children's bedrooms. That way, if something is dirty when you undress the kids at night, you can spray that stain straight-away rather than waiting for laundry day. A real clothes-saver!

Socks

Turn them right-side out before washing in warm water and machine drying. Sometimes I'll see people do the wash and socks will come out of the dryer all rolled up into big wads, and I'll think, Now how in the world are they ever going to get clean? They can't get clean unless you undo them. So just make sure that you do.

T-Shirts and Cotton Dresses

Wash these in cold water with like colors. T-shirts wrinkle like you wouldn't believe, so before you go on a trip, sprinkle them with a bit of water, roll them up, and put them in a plastic bag; by the time you get to your hotel they'll be ready to be ironed and will press up really nicely because they'll be evenly damp. If it's a long trip, though, that trick could cause a musty smell, so only use it if you'll arrive at your destination within four hours or so. To get your white T-shirts really white, air-fluff them, then hang them on the line in the sun rather than putting them in the dryer. The sun is a natural whitening agent.

Sweatpants and Sweatshirts

Wash these in cold water with like colors; then air-fluff and air-dry.

Workout Wear

My kids were always doing some kind of athletics after school, so washing sports bras was part of my routine. Toss the ones with underwire in a zippered mesh bag and wash in cold water. Then air-dry to avoid shrinkage. Never put sports bras in the dryer, which will quickly ruin the elastic (and likely mess with the snaps and such too).

TENDING to OUTERWEAR and ACCESSORIES

Down-Filled Jackets

Wash kids' jackets in warm water (be sure to zip them up first) with mild detergent—regular detergent can strip feathers of their oils. Slip a few golf balls into a sock, tie up the top, and put the sock in the dryer with the jackets to keep the filling from getting displaced. For larger, adult jackets, the agitator in front-loading washers can sometimes be too harsh, so unless you have one of those new front-loaders, hand-wash in cold water.

Fleece Pullovers

To keep them soft and pill-free, wash in cold water with mild detergent, air-fluff, then hang the garments across multiple clotheslines that run parallel to one other.

Hats, Gloves, and Scarves

Hats, gloves, and scarves—whether cotton, wool, or acrylic—can be tossed in the wash. Hand-wash cashmere. Use cold water and dry these items flat so that they keep their shape. You can hand-wash leather work gloves in warm, sudsy water, turning them inside out after a few minutes to get every part good and clean. Dry them flat, occasionally massaging the leather with your hands so that it doesn't dry too stiff. When they're almost dry, put the gloves on for a minute or two to reshape them. For your nice leather gloves, however, stick to wiping them with a cloth that's been soaked in soapy water and wrung until damp.

WASTE NOT WANT NOT

Dry-clean only? Sure, some things must be taken to the cleaners. Like a nice wool coat. But I don't like putting harsh chemicals on my clothes unless it's absolutely necessary. So I would venture to say that you can probably get by with hand washing most things that say "dry-clean only." Even a casmere sweater can be hand-washed with mild detergent and dried flat. Plus, it'll cost you to dry-clean something, so if the garment isn't too precious, why not try hand washing?

Leather Handbags, Belts, and Shoes

You can't wash these in the washer because the leather may bleed; they'll need to be spot-cleaned. For shoes, make sure they're dry and free of mud and then apply shoe cream (same color as the shoes) with a soft cloth. Let them sit overnight. Then apply a wax polish, rubbing in small circles before buffing with a horsehair brush.

GETTING FANCY ABOUT FOOTWEAR

Sneakers

Slip leather or canvas sneakers inside clean white socks to minimize scuff marks (this way, there's no need to remove the laces, which would otherwise wrap around the washer's agitator). This will also cut down on that annoying noise you get from shoes banging around in the washer; add a towel or two to muffle the sound even more. Wash sneakers in cold water, then air-dry them.

Slippers

You'll need to check your labels, but many slippers, even those with rubber soles, can be tossed in the washer on cold. Air-dry them.

Flip-Flops

Wash these in the machine with cold water, or just do as I do and wear them in the shower now and then. Rub the soles with soap and a rag to get out any ground-in dirt. Then place them outside in the sun to dry.

TREATING **TEXTILES**

Sheets and Pillowcases

Since these are in close contact with your skin, wash them once a week—and more frequently if someone has been sick. Wash cotton, cotton blends, flannel, synthetics, or bamboo (so trendy!) in hot water to kill bacteria; dry them on low. Remember to fold sheets right away so wrinkles won't set in. Hand-wash linen, silk, or sateen sheets in cold water with mild detergent and air-dry until slightly damp. Then make the bed with them, and they'll finish drying with virtually no wrinkles.

Washing Blankets and Pillows

Machine-wash cotton blankets in warm water. Wash wool with mild detergent and cold water on the gentle cycle. Spin both types in the washer until the excess moisture is all soaked up. Gently stretch the blankets back to their original sizes (measure first if you're not sure what that is) before air drying.

As for pillows: Unless your pillow tags say "dry-clean only," you can wash them in the machine every three to six months on the gentlest cycle; use warm water and a bit of mild detergent. I run pillows through the rinse cycle twice to get all the detergent off. Air-dry.

Drying Blankets and Comforters

Place them in the dryer for just a few minutes to fluff up, and then hang heavy comforters, quilts, and wool blankets on several clotheslines that run alongside one another rather than just one, to balance out the weight so the items won't stretch out and no stitches will be forced out. And don't forget to clean your clotheslines before each use with a damp rag (you never know when a bird did a number on them). To be extra careful, drape an old sheet over the lines and place your goods on top of it. And put a sheet above them while they're on the line; birds have no respect.

my **HOUSE**, my **RULES**

I always **ENLISTED THE BOYS** to help me hang clothes on the line—**TIM** and **TOM ESPECIALLY**, because they were the oldest. I was **PREGNANT** most of the time, so it was hard to bend over to grab stuff out of the basket. They'd hand me the garments **ONE BY ONE**, and I'd pin everything to the line. That way I could stay **UPRIGHT** and get the **JOB DONE** much faster.

Quilts

You can put these in the washer on the gentle cycle, but make sure to use cold water and mild soap, because you don't want to mess up any stitching. If you have a homemade quilt, you don't want to wash it too often or it'll get ruined. Once a year or so is fine; put painter's tape on the back with the date that you last washed it so that you'll know when it's time. Another thing you can do is the smell test: If it has a musty odor, it's time for a wash. One more thing: If your quilt is an heirloom, don't wash it yourself. Spend the money to have it professionally cleaned.

my HOUSE, my RULES

Never cover up with a **SPECIAL QUILT**—pull it off before hopping into bed or it's just not going to last. It's basically just for **LOOKING AT.** I am making each of my grandchildren a quilt (that is my goal—seeing as how I have **TWENTY-TWO** of them, I'd better get cracking). I'll **WRITE** each a nice little poem about HOW TO CARE FOR IT.

WASTE NOT WANT NOT

We all love the fresh scent that dryer sheets leave behind. Here's another trick to keep fabrics baby-bottom soft: Add a quarter cup of baking soda to the wash cycle or a tablespoon of white vinegar to the rinse cycle. Soft and heavenly!

Mattress Pads

Wash these once a month (unless they're soiled, then wash them right away!) in hot water; air-dry. Doctors may order allergy sufferers and asthmatics to wash them more frequently.

Shower Curtains

Whether they're plastic, vinyl, or cloth, wash them in the machine in cold water with your towels. The towels will rub against them and help get that soap scum and slime off, especially with plastic and vinyl curtains. Shake them before you put them in the dryer. Then dry them for a few minutes, just to get the wrinkles out (and so vinyl curtains won't melt; one time I left one in for an hour and got a hole melted right in the middle). Then hang them on the line and they'll dry really nicely.

Towels

Try to use towels at least three or four times before washing them in warm or hot water. Toss them in the dryer, but you might want to consider skipping the fabric softener; the chemicals in it can stiffen them.

Rugs

Wash small cotton or synthetic rugs and bath mats, even those with rubber or latex backings, in cold water on the gentle cycle. Air-dry.

Curtains

Cotton curtains can be washed in cold water; air-dry them, then iron when they're slightly damp to get out those wrinkles before they set in.

Tablecloths and Napkins

If one of your dinner guests spills greasy gravy on your tablecloth, don't fret. Just soak those soiled textiles in ice water overnight. In the morning, throw them in the washer and use warm water. Oily stains are tough to get out, and the dryer will set them. So bring the napkins or tablecloths to a bright spot to look for marks; if stains remain, repeat the washing process, then hang on the line to dry.

my HOUSE, my RULES

Everything seems to be all "BIGGER IS BETTER" these days. Well, I just don't agree. Do you ever see those HUGE bath towels hanging in people's BATHROOMS? Who needs them? They cost so much to launder and take so much time to dry. A waste of time, SPACE, and energy. I say just make sure your towels are large enough to DRY YOU WELL. NO BIG TOWELS in my house.

DEALING with
DELICATES

Fine Bras and Lingerie

For your fancy lacy or silky little numbers, use baby detergent, mild soap, or shampoo, and hand-wash in cool water; just swish the water a bit, gently dip the garments up and down, and let them soak for a few minutes. Since these are worn close to the skin, where they absorb oils and the like, you should ideally wash them immediately after wearing. Rather than wringing them out, gently roll the lingerie in a thick towel to get out any excess water and lay them flat to dry. Sometimes I'll bring stuff in the shower with me and wash it right there. Kills two birds with one stone.

Everyday Bras and Lingerie

You can wash your day-to-day unmentionables in the machine; just be sure to place them in a zippered mesh bag for protection and fasten the ends together so that they don't get tangled in the bag. Putting them in the bag will also remind you not to throw these delicates in the dryer; hang them on the line instead. If you see any perspiration stains, rub them with a bar of soap and presoak in sudsy water. And don't put bras in with heavier items. Just wash them on their own, so that the weight of other things doesn't disfigure them.

Underwear

Turn your panties inside out to make sure you get them really clean. Wash them in hot water and toss them in the dryer to kill any remaining germs. Or hang them in the sun, but don't leave them there all day—too much sunlight can discolor them.

Pantyhose

Hand-wash these in cool water with a drop of detergent. Or you can machine-wash them on the gentle cycle, then toss them in the spin cycle to get out all that excess moisture before hanging them on the line. It's much easier for them to dry that way. And rather than drain the water out of the sink after hand washing, I'll use it to water my plants.

Swimsuits

Rinse swim gear right away in cold water to make sure that chlorine and other nasty stuff gets out quickly and doesn't fade the garment or affect the elasticity. Because who wants a dull, sagging swimsuit? (Sometimes I just marched the kids straight into the shower with their suits on.) Hand-wash the suits in cold water and mild detergent and spin them dry. Finish by line-drying in the shade.

With **FOUR GIRLS** in the mix, we needed three clotheslines. The middle one was designated for the UNMENTIONABLES. I'd hang the sheets on the two exterior lines so that our LINGERIE was protected from neighbors' eyes. No PEEPING TOMS allowed.

WASHING BABY CLOTHES

When you buy baby clothes or receive them as a gift, it's best to wash them before baby wears them. Don't ever use harsh detergent; onesies and the like should be washed with a mild detergent just for kids. Baby detergent is formulated to leave fabric soft, and the good ones don't contain additives prone to cause irritation. Make sure to pretreat stains like drool or formula so that they don't set; soak the clothes in a pan of cold water and a drop or two of detergent, and work through the stains with a soft-bristle nylon brush. Here's how to treat the specific offenders:

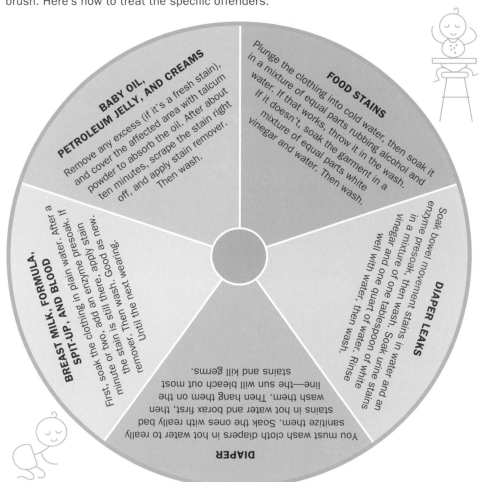

BABY OIL, PETROLEUM JELLY, AND CREAMS
Remove any excess (if it's a fresh stain), and cover the affected area with talcum powder to absorb the oil. After about ten minutes, scrape the stain right off, and apply stain remover. Then wash.

FOOD STAINS
Plunge the clothing into cold water, then soak it in a mixture of equal parts rubbing alcohol and water. If that works, throw it in the wash. If it doesn't, soak the garment in a mixture of equal parts white vinegar and water. Then wash.

DIAPER LEAKS
Soak bowel movement stains in water and enzyme presoak, then wash. Soak urine stains in a mixture of one tablespoon of white vinegar and one quart of water. Rinse well with water, then wash.

DIAPER
You must wash cloth diapers in hot water to really sanitize them. Soak the ones with really bad stains in hot water and borax first, then wash them. Then hang them on the line—the sun will bleach out most stains and kill germs.

BREAST MILK, FORMULA, SPIT-UP, AND BLOOD
First, soak the clothing in an enzyme presoak. If the stain is still there, add an enzyme stain remover. Then wash. Good as new. After a minute or two, wash. Good as new. Until the next wearing.

MY **MESSY** BOYS

REPEAT

CLEAN TOMMY → **TIMMY SPITS UP** → **CLEAN TIMMY**

My kids went through their share of spit-up stages. I can still smell that smell, too. But to get those stains out, I never used bleach. If the clothes turned yellow, I just endured it. And I always used a towel or a cloth diaper on my shoulder to protect my clothes. But if you want to talk real messes, try having twins.

TOMMY is HUNGRY

FEED TIMMY ← **TIMMY is HUNGRY** ← **FEED TOMMY**

CHANGE TOMMY

The minute Tommy was cleaned up, sparkling and ready for a day out, Timmy would spit up all over his shirt. By the time I got Timmy clean, Tommy would need to be fed. Then Timmy. Then changing. We went from the babies' room to the laundry room to the kitchen and back again.

CHANGE TIMMY → **TOMMY SPITS UP**

GETTING **IRONING STRAIGHT**

I love to iron and had great fun teaching my girls to do it. I started them on hankies, because hankies are often 100 percent cotton, so they get nice and wrinkly. Here are a few things I told them about ironing:

You must keep the iron moving—don't let it sit or you'll get burn marks.

Use both hands at once—one to iron, the other to keep smoothing your garment as you go.

Iron dark-colored items on the wrong side so you don't get those shiny marks.

If there's something that you just can't iron right away, like a cotton shirt, say, sprinkle it with a little water and put it in the refrigerator or the deep freeze so mold and mildew won't form. It'll stay nice and fresh until you're ready to deal with it. I used to do this as a kid with my mom; we'd take a quart jar, poke holes in the lid with nails, then fill the jar with water and sprinkle things that way. Sprinkling works well on cotton, linen, rayon, and silk; synthetic fabrics can often be ironed when dry, though it's still best to iron when the clothes are right out of the dryer.

There are some things you just shouldn't iron—knit sweaters, for instance. Just shake them out when they're still damp, lay them on the ironing board, and press the wrinkles out with your hands.

Only iron clothes that have been washed; ironing soiled ones may set a stain.

You want to make sure you get a nice, secure, slick ironing-board cover. If it's too loose or soft, it can be difficult to iron on. Mine has a foil back, too, which is ideal because it absorbs heat and reflects it back onto the clothes.

To really get out those wrinkles, use the steam setting. It's great for tablecloths, shirts, and hankies. But if you're like me, you may have had a problem with steam in the past. You know: It can mess you up by putting spots on your clothes when the calcium that builds up comes out of the steam holes. So always be careful not to shake the iron too much when you're steaming. And press the steam button a few times with the iron pointed away from you to clear the vents of any buildup.

IRONING CLOTHING and LINENS

Button-Down Shirts

Make sure that cotton and linen shirts are damp for the best results. (You can fill a spray bottle with water just for this purpose!) Iron the collar first (the wrong side, then the right side), going from the pointy part inward. Crease the collar with your hand, not the iron. Then put each sleeve on the board and do the cuffs and sleeves—both sides. Place the body of the shirt on the board and press that, wrong side first. Never iron over buttons or they may crack or melt; they can also scratch your iron. Just sneak the nose of the iron in around them. If you like, use spray starch on the collars to keep the dirt from penetrating.

Pants

When ironing pants, whether cotton or synthetic, try to crease them the way they originally were. Make sure you iron the front crease first, because that's most noticeable. So make it nice and crisp, and then the back one will just fall into place. That's what I do with my khaki pedal pushers.

WASTE NOT WANT NOT Don't overheat your clothes. Some things need a hot iron, like really wrinkly cotton and linen, but in general you can get away with using the lowest setting. Heating the iron too high is a waste of energy and harsh on fabrics too.

Silk Ties

Using a low heat and the delicates setting, lay a clean cloth over the tie and iron down the length of it on the wrong side.

Tablecloths

Use a steam iron on tablecloths to get them really crisp. For embroidered tablecloths, iron them on the wrong side so that the back gets very flat and the embroidery on the front gets raised. It looks so pretty that way. And if you iron the top you risk catching some of the delicate embroidery. So that the ends of the tablecloth don't hit the floor and get dirty, place a sheet under the board. For round cloths, start at the center and work your way out.

MAINTAINING the
LAUNDRY ROOM

Emptying the Dryer's Lint Trap

Each time you take a load out, empty the lint trap; the dryer is so much more efficient that way. Even if there's just a little bit of dust in there, swipe it clean with your hand. It's a waste of energy not to.

Cleaning the Dryer's Vent

Every month, use your vacuum's brush attachment to clean the vent.

Sanitizing the Washer

It may seem odd that an appliance that's used for cleaning needs to be cleaned, but it's true. About once a month, run a cleansing rinse cycle by filling the washer with hot water and one cup of white vinegar to get off any grime left on the interior walls. And to keep mold and mildew at bay, leave the lid open for half an hour after each wash.

Tackling the
Washer's and Dryer's Exteriors

Wipe down the exteriors and insides of the doors every now and then with a little dishwashing liquid and warm water. And don't forget the knobs. Get in there with a toothbrush or cotton swab if you need to.

Cleaning a Sticky Iron

If your iron isn't sliding over clothes as smoothly as it used to, check for nasty spots. If you find some, here's what you do: Sprinkle some coarse salt on a clean cloth and run a hot iron over it; the salt will help remove all that grime. You can also try running the iron over wax paper. That'll do the trick, too.

WASTE NOT WANT NOT It's very important to launder stains right away, even if you have to do a special small load. Saving nice clothing is worth using a little extra energy, I think. My son Tom worked on a pig farm as a teenager, and he'd come inside with the stinkiest, dirtiest shirts around, so I'd make sure to get to them quick.

TRANSLATING CLOTHING
LABELS

Deciphering the labels on tags means being able to read in a different language. Here's what all those strange-looking symbols mean:

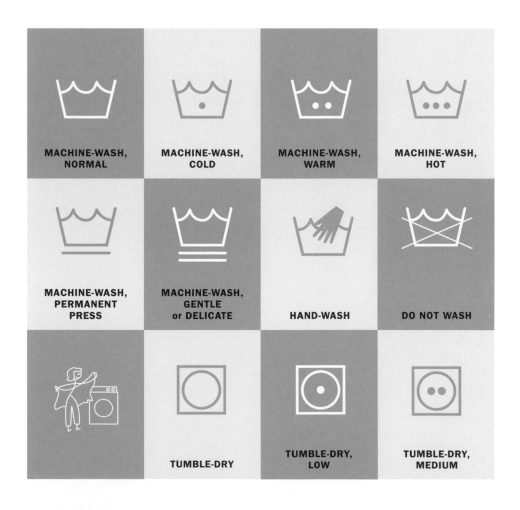

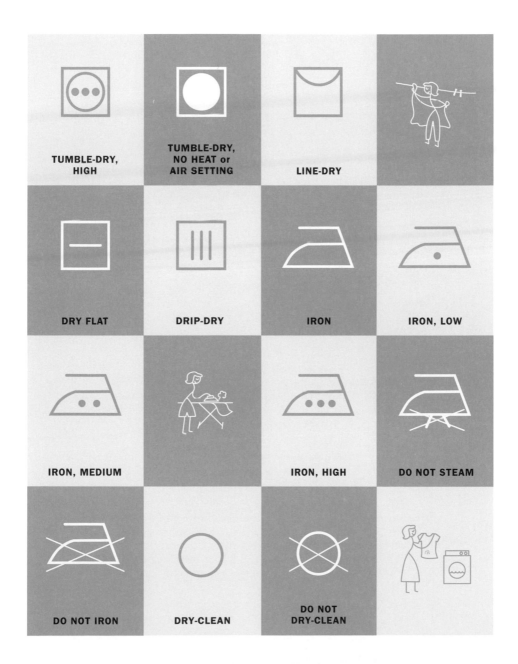

TUMBLE-DRY, HIGH

TUMBLE-DRY, NO HEAT or AIR SETTING

LINE-DRY

DRY FLAT

DRIP-DRY

IRON

IRON, LOW

IRON, MEDIUM

IRON, HIGH

DO NOT STEAM

DO NOT IRON

DRY-CLEAN

DO NOT DRY-CLEAN

TACKLING STAINS IN A FLASH

Mishaps happen. But there's no need to cry over spilled milk, wine, or juice. Just follow my get-it-out guidelines and you'll be spotless in no time.

CHOCOLATE	With nine kids, you bet chocolate was going to end up on something. When the candy bar makes a scene, take a spatula to scrape off as much as possible, then soak the garment in cold water for half an hour before rubbing it with laundry detergent and tossing it in the wash.
BLOOD	My kids were big on sports, so there were a lot of skinned knees. Use an eyedropper to put a few drops of hydrogen peroxide on bloodstained garments before washing them. If you're away from home, spit on the spot—you heard me right. Saliva has an enzyme that breaks down the proteins in blood. You learn something new every day!
RED FRUIT JUICE	For pesky stains like this, grab your teakettle, boil some water, then pour it over the affected area. Or squeeze a fresh lemon right on the spot—that works well, too.
CRAYON	Kids get crayon on everything. Here's how to get a wax stain out: Toss that shirt or sweater in the freezer until the stain hardens, then place a paper towel on top of the spot and iron it until the color transfers onto the paper. Like magic!
GRASS	Grass stains are easy, thankfully. Dab the spots with rubbing alcohol and soak the clothes in hot water. Good as new.
GREASE	We kept our maroon station wagon for ten years. It wasn't the most modern means of transportation, so it would leave a grease stain on someone's pant leg or shirt now and then when clothes got caught in a door. I didn't worry when it happened and neither should you; just rub a little cornmeal into the stain to absorb it, let it sit for a few minutes, then brush the powder and the stain away and wash as usual.
RUST	Squeeze lemon juice onto the stain, sprinkle some salt onto it, then place the garment outside in the sun for a few hours before washing.

MASCARA	Teenage girls can be challenging, but mascara stains are easy: Mix a tablespoon of dishwashing liquid with two cups cold water, apply the solution to the stain, and then blot until it's gone.
RED WINE	I keep a spray bottle filled with club soda just for situations like this. After saturating the stain, simply blot it with a paper towel. If the stain remains, toss the garment in the sink for a half an hour or so with water and borax. Brand-spanking new.
SOY SAUCE	Soak the stain in cold water, dab a bit of detergent on it, then launder as usual. It comes out quick.
BEER	Blot the spot with a mixture of white vinegar and water.
CHEWING GUM	When sticky substances like this make their way onto your clothes, place an ice cube in a plastic bag (so that it doesn't drip), then apply it to the spot until it freezes. Afterward, use a spatula or a dull knife to scrape the stuff away.
COFFEE	My morning coffee sometimes lands in my lap. When it does, I soak my slacks in warm water and borax for about half an hour, then launder them in hot water.
INK	Place the garment stain-side-down on a paper towel, then blot the back with rubbing alcohol until the stain seeps from the shirt onto the towel. It's fun to watch!
MILK	This isn't so bad. Just dab the spot with warm water and apply some stain remover, then wash as usual.
PERSPIRATION	If it's a fresh stain, pour shampoo on the soiled area before washing. If it's an old stain, apply white vinegar, rinse, then launder the garment in the hottest water safe for the fabric. You can also try soaking whites overnight in oxygen bleach. Whenever possible, I recommend hanging white clothing in the sun to dry. Sunshine is nature's incredible bleach!

LAUNDRY ROOM
MANIA

My laundry room is located smack-dab in between the garage and the kitchen. You have to trek through it to get into the main part of the house, which made it a handy place for the kids to shed their hats and mittens before coming in. And that barrel of woolly things made an appealing spot for our various pets.

When Teresa was little, she came running into the living room, wearing these cute little purple overalls, screaming "Mom, mom! The cat's pooping kitties! The cat's pooping kitties!" Well, it turns out that this old gray stray cat that we had found in the yard one day—I don't even know if we ever named her—had a litter of four kittens right in our mitten barrel! I peeked into that big barrel, afraid of what I might see. I found the mother cat surrounded by her brand-new kittens, all cozy and comfy on our mittens. What a delight.

We put the kittens in old shoe boxes and kept them in the shed out back. The kids played with them day and night. Chasing them around, cuddling them every which way. And that little mama cat watched, calm and proud.

But it wasn't always peaceful at our house with all those animals around. When Maria was four, she kept her hamster in a metal cage in the laundry room. She loved that little guy and decided that he should get to enjoy some freedom. Unbeknownst to me, she opened the door of the cage and let him out. Suddenly, Maria ran to me, screaming, "The cat's got my hamster! The cat's got my hamster!" That old cat had the hamster hanging out of her mouth!

Suddenly, my Granger house turned into an action movie. There I was, chasing the cat with the hamster in her mouth around the house while my four-year-old trailed close behind and the other kids watched, wide-eyed. Finally I got my hands on the cat and shook her until she finally let go of that hamster. The hamster was a bit shocked and none too pleased about his little ride around the house, but he survived. And Maria never "set him free" again, that's for sure.

CHAPTER 7

CLEAN
NOOKS and CRANNIES

Every house needs some good nooks and crannies to act as catchalls and storage areas. Some homes have more than others, but there are ways to carve them out where they didn't exist before. That's what Vern did. In the dining area off the kitchen he built us a cupboard, with a door that pulls down to reveal the sewing machine. ⟶

It was the perfect location: I could listen to the stove and washer while watching the kids. And then I'd be able to put everything back quickly, too. I would just stuff all the sewing materials into a box and hide it, and the dining table would be clear for a meal. It looks like a regular cabinet when it's closed up—you can't tell at all that a sewing center is tucked away in there.

Another of my favorite nooks in our house is right under the sewing area—the crawl space. That's where I stash all my tomatoes, beans, and carrots after canning, because it's nice and cool—but not cold enough to freeze everything. The kids used to love going under the house to get me my canned goods. But that crawl space isn't just great for canning—it can also protect you from the elements. When Monica graduated from nurse's training, around 1978, she got a new car and wanted us to drive with her to Ohio to see her college friend. So we did just that—and left Teresa at home with her four siblings and boyfriend, Roger, who was visiting. Teresa and Roger happened to be outside when a big storm came up and part of a tree broke off and fell onto the clotheslines. They were so afraid for their lives that they crawled underneath the house. So nooks and crannies may surprise you with their dual functionality. And keeping them clean is essential.

the **MUDROOMS, ENTRYWAYS, and HALLWAYS** 177

making the ENTRYWAY or MUDROOM FUNCTIONAL 177

cleaning WELCOME MATS 177

handling the HALLS 177

ERASING FINGERPRINTS from WALLS 177

keeping your ART BEAUTIFUL 178

the **STAIRS** 179

vacuuming the STAIRS 179

getting FINGERPRINTS off BANISTERS 179

the **ATTIC** 179

SETTING UP your ATTIC 179

VENTILATING your ATTIC 179

ORGANIZING your ATTIC 180

CLEANING your ATTIC 180

DEHUMIDIFYING CRAWL SPACES 180

the BASEMENT 180
ORGANIZING your BASEMENT 180
DEHUMIDIFYING your BASEMENT 180
CLEANING your BASEMENT 180

the CLOSETS 181
ORGANIZING a CLOTHES CLOSET 181
STORING CLOTHES 182
the LINEN CLOSET 183
MOTHPROOFING your clothes 184
UTILITY closets 185

the SECRETS of SEWING 186
putting together a SEWING KIT 186
sewing on REPLACEMENT BUTTONS 187
sneaky SEWING TIPS 187

TOOLBOX

BRUSHES
Counter
Scrub
Toothbrush

BUCKETS, GLOVES, and MORE
Bucket or pail
Dustpan
Rubber gloves
Spray bottle

CLEANING PRODUCTS
All-purpose cleaning liquid
Baby wipes
Baking soda
Dishwashing liquid
Glass cleaner
Mild laundry detergent
Rubbing alcohol
White vinegar

CLOTHS, RAGS, SPONGES, and OTHER WIPERS
Chamois cloth
Cotton balls and/or swabs
Dust cloth
Extendable duster
Lint-free cloth
Microfiber cloth
Muslin
Soft cloth
Polishing cloth

SWEEPING, MOPPING, and VACUUMING
Angled broom
Dust mop
Floor mop
Handheld vacuum cleaner
Push broom
Stick vacuum
Vacuum *with attachments*

ODOR FIXERS
Lemon

WAXING and POLISHING
Furniture polish
Furniture wax
Metal polish
Olive oil
Paste wax

HANDY to HAVE THESE AROUND
Compressed air
Correction fluid
Slice of white bread
Toothpaste

the MUDROOMS, ENTRYWAYS, and HALLWAYS

Making the Entryway or Mudroom Functional

Since the family shuffles in here, you'll need to outfit the space with organizational essentials or else it'll easily turn into a mess. There are a few things that really make this space work well: coatracks, for keeping everything on the wall and off the floor; a boot tray, to stop people from traipsing through the house in wet footwear (a metal cookie sheet works, too); and a bench, for sitting down to put on or take off shoes. One with a lift-up top is great, because you can store towels or blankets inside. Or fruit. I don't have a grocery store in town, so I try to shop for the entire week and sometimes I have so much extra fruit that I'll put it inside my bench. The other day I found wrinkled apples in there.

Cleaning Welcome Mats

Shake them out once a week to remove dust and dirt, then vacuum them. I've made the mistake of buying cheap, thin welcome mats, and you know what happens when you buy flimsy ones? The wind blows them away. Not so welcoming. Get nice, sturdy coir (a natural fiber) mats, thick ones that will stay put. You can place thinner, more decorative ones inside. Place welcome mats at all entrances; they will greatly reduce the amount of dirt that gets ground into your pretty floors.

Handling the Halls

Sweep if you have flooring, vacuum if you have carpeting, and whatever you do, try not to hit those white baseboards! If you do get a smudge, here's an easy touch-up trick: Dab the spot with correction fluid.

Erasing Fingerprints from Walls

Little hands tend to touch walls a lot, getting stubborn dirt and grease on your nice paint job. Don't scrub those walls with hot, soapy water, however: You might find that you'll remove more paint than fingerprints! Instead, try a baby wipe, which will make quick work of those little smudges. Another little-known secret: If you get dirt or grease on your wallpaper, a slice of white bread—with its absorbent powers—can miraculously make it disappear.

KEEPING YOUR ART BEAUTIFUL

It's important to pretty up your nooks and crannies—whether you line a stairway with framed prints or hang a painting above a window seat. In our entryway, we have a stained-glass window that Maria made; it's beautiful and fills the space with color. We have lots of framed family photos on the walls too. Here's how to keep all of your pieces looking lovely.

Choose the location for the artwork carefully. Direct sunlight can cause your precious photographs to fade. If you can't find a dimly lit spot, keep your drapes drawn.

Don't hang your artwork near a fireplace—soot and smoke will dirty it.

Mold is the enemy of artwork. Hang your prized pieces in your driest rooms.

Once a week, dust paintings and photographs with a paintbrush.

Once a year, clean glass-front paintings and photographs. Don't spray window or glass cleaner directly onto the piece—too risky. Instead, put cleaner on a cloth that's barely damp and wipe the glass. Try to avoid touching the frame.

Keep your paws off the artwork. Our fingers have oils in them that can cause damage.

Clean metal frames with an all-purpose liquid cleaner and a soft cloth. Wipe lacquered wood frames with a dry, lint-free cloth.

the STAIRS

Vacuuming the Stairs

Do this about once a week. If you're strapped for time, just focus on the middle section of each step—that's where people tend to walk. Instead of lugging a huge, heavy vacuum cleaner up and down, use a light-weight stick vacuum that doesn't need to be plugged in. Even if you don't have carpeted stairs, a weekly stick vacuum should do the job.

Getting Fingerprints off Banisters

Use equal parts white vinegar and water on wood, and dishwashing liquid and water on metal. Dry thoroughly.

the ATTIC

Setting Up Your Attic

Avoid covering any of the walls up there with plastic—that'll just trap heat and moisture. Drape any furnishings with cloths to protect them from dust. If you can line unfinished floors with plywood, do; it's safer to walk on.

Ventilating Your Attic

Making sure your attic is ventilated is a good way to keep your whole house cool because the attic is where a lot of your home's heat enters. Get a professional to help you place exhaust vents high and intake vents low.

my **HOUSE,** my **RULES**

I like to keep all of my **GIFT-WRAPPING** supplies in one spot. Consider setting up an area in a **CORNER OF THE GARAGE** or a section of the home office so that everything you need to wrap a gift for a **KID'S BIRTHDAY PARTY** or a **HOUSEWARMING** will be within easy reach. All you need is a nice **DESK SURFACE** with a wall behind it. Toss wrapping paper rolls into a large **VASE** on the floor. You can hang a pegboard **BEHIND THE DESK**, then attach hooks to it for scissors, **TAPE,** and spools of ribbon, and have clear **BOXES** for holding tape, ribbons, and bows.

Organizing Your Attic

It's important to make it easy to find the stuff you stash up there. Label boxes according to their contents, with very large letters in black permanent marker, and keep the boxes you need access to most frequently closest to the door. I keep baby shoes, baby dresses, and baptismal dresses in our attic. But our attic is just a crawl space, so you can't stand up in it. I crawl in there and have Vern hand me stuff, but I'm realizing that I can't get in and out very easily anymore, so it'll soon be off-limits for me.

Cleaning Your Attic

During your spring cleaning and fall storing, go ahead and vacuum your attic with a stick vacuum. Don't go too crazy trying to get it to sparkle (who has time?), but keeping the dust levels down makes it more pleasant when you need to get up there to find something.

Dehumidifying Crawl Spaces

For small areas with humidity problems, fasten a rubber band around a dozen pieces of chalk and cover the band with ribbon. Hang this from a hook. The chalk will absorb excess moisture.

the BASEMENT

Organizing Your Basement

This part of the house is great for storing things, but it's also prone to flooding. So keep your valuables on high shelves, just in case. Things you often need access to can be kept near the floor as long as they're up on something, like cinder blocks. Better safe than sorry. Avoid having carpets and rugs on the basement floor. The moisture will turn them moldy. Best to stick to bare floors. Don't use cardboard boxes to store anything precious. It's better to keep your valuables in waterproof, see-through plastic bins.

Dehumidifying Your Basement

Basements can get very humid, which can lead to mold, mildew, and rust. An electronic dehumidifier can remove excess moisture and help to control mustiness and odors, although these also can produce heat.

Cleaning Your Basement

If you have an unfinished basement that you only use for storage, vacuum and dust about once a month. A lot of people I know have finished basements, which are great for when you have kids, especially teenagers. If your family is spending a lot of time down there, care for it as you would any living room: Once a week, vacuum the floors and upholstery and dust any surfaces and electronics. And just like your living room: No eating down there! Crumbs can invite pests.

the CLOSETS

Organizing a Clothes Closet

If you have a small bedroom closet, carve out space by moving out-of-season stuff into a storage room. If you're lucky enough to have ample space, go through the closet twice a year and create four piles: trash (anything permanently stained or ripped), donations (anything you haven't worn in a year), and things to keep (put aside anything that needs care, like a shirt with a missing button or a stained skirt). Look for ways that you can implement organizational solutions, too. Attach hooks to the walls for holding purses and scarves. Consider using thinner hangers to maximize space, or a hanging shoe rack or sweater bags. Try sorting your clothes by color; it'll be easier to put together outfits in the morning, and you just might find out that you have one too many black blouses. As for shoes, I place empty soda bottles in my boots to keep them standing up straight.

my **HOUSE,** my **RULES**

Closets might be the best nooks and **CRANNIES** of all. I like to have each closet in my home serve its own DISTINCT PURPOSE. The closet in the living room behind the **BOOKCASE** is for holding toys, tractors, and books for when my grandkids visit, and **OTHERS** are just dedicated to old balls or hard hats. I have one closet behind the **FAMILY ROOM** that houses the furnace, along with BASEBALL bats, sleeping bags, and snack sets—it's a great **CATCHALL**. And I have another closet for umbrellas, our **FLAG,** and little gifts that I might need for my bridge girls. Every now and then, ESPECIALLY with my clothes closets, I like to go through them. Sometimes I'll think, Well, I haven't worn this in I can't remember how long. And then I **DONATE** it to someone who can really benefit from it. Because I obviously don't need it if I can't even remember the last time I used it.

STORING CLOTHES

Take good care of your clothes, even when you store them for a season or two (or in the case of your wedding dress, many seasons!). And don't keep them in the plastic from the dry cleaner. Any moisture trapped inside may cause mildew.

FUR AND LEATHER COATS AND JACKETS: These need to breathe, so don't store them in plastic bags or bins. Instead, place them in old pillowcases or sheets.

CASHMERE AND WOOL SWEATERS: Wrap your sweaters in white acid-free tissue paper and store them in a cedar chest or a box with cedar chips to deter moths.

SILK TOPS AND DRESSES: Fold these delicate clothes carefully and wrap them in white acid-free tissue paper. Store them in a cedar chest or a box with cedar chips to keep them fresh.

LEATHER BAGS: Don't hang your nice pocketbooks by the handles! They'll lose their shape. Instead, set them on a shelf.

JEANS: Just fold and stack them. Hang pairs you like to wear for dressy occasions so that they won't wrinkle.

SUITS: Store these in cloth garment bags.

WEDDING OR FORMAL DRESSES: After having these professionally cleaned, wrap them in white acid-free tissue paper and place them in sealed boxes in a cool, dry location.

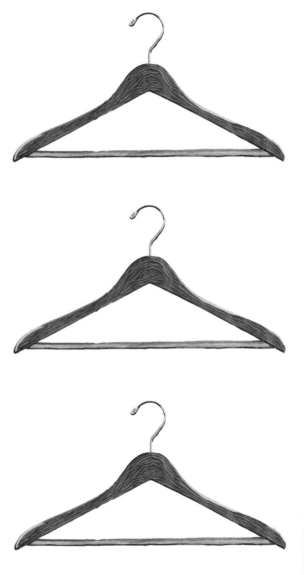

THE LINEN CLOSET

A linen closet full of freshly washed sheets and towels is a great delight. In a busy house, it's important to be ready for anything, even surprise overnight guests. Always have at least one spare set of sheets and two extra towels. Don't throw out old towels and sheets: Old towels are perfect for drying off your pet after a bath; old sheets can be used as drop cloths. They can go in the garage, basement, or attic. Be sure to keep the linens that you need to store in protective, mothproof bags. Here's how to stay as organized as possible.

TABLE LINENS: Group tablecloths by size and napkins by type, like cocktail or dinner. Keep holiday items together so you can reach in and grab what you need.

BLANKETS: Sort by bedroom. The heaviest-weight blanket should be at the bottom; the lightest at the top.

TOWELS: Sort by kind of towel: beach towels, bath towels, hand towels, and washcloths. Put just washed towels on the bottom of the pile so that every towel gets even use.

SHEETS: Here's a handy trick: Place each set of sheets inside one of its pillowcases so everything stays together. Group the sheets by bedroom. Put the most recently washed sheets on the bottom and use from the top.

COMFORTERS: Wash your comforters (including down comforters) and hang dry before you store. For these, be sure not to use cedar or camphor—your down comforters will retain the smell forever. Store them on a shelf in loose cloths or plastic bags.

WASTE NOT WANT NOT What's the use of having spare buttons if you can never find the one you want? String same-color buttons on dental floss and tie the ends together; keep the strand in a box. And don't throw away those extra buttons just because they've seen better days. Paint them with clear nail polish and they'll look shiny and new.

MOTHPROOFING
YOUR CLOTHES

Moths are the scourge of stored clothing and blankets. Keeping your clothes fresh and clean—especially woolens—is your best defense. Moth eggs hatch into fabric, and the larvae feed on embedded dirt and perspiration. But even if you keep your clothes clean, larvae still can lurk. Try one of these treatments.

LAVENDER

Lavender not only smells wonderful, it's a great way to repel moths. Tuck sachets of it into your drawers or hang them in closets.

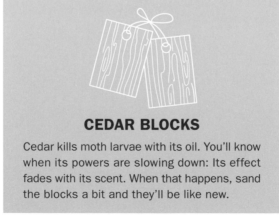

CEDAR BLOCKS

Cedar kills moth larvae with its oil. You'll know when its powers are slowing down: Its effect fades with its scent. When that happens, sand the blocks a bit and they'll be like new.

UTILITY CLOSETS

Here's what I keep in my utility closet year-round. Just make sure to store all the cleaning supplies on a high shelf, not under the sink, where little hands can reach.

- ☐ **Key rack** (with labels, of course!)
- ☐ **Batteries**
- ☐ **Flashlights**
- ☐ **Dust cloths**
- ☐ **Polishing cloths**
- ☐ **Metal polish**

- ☐ **Furniture polish**
- ☐ **Furniture wax**
- ☐ **Stand-up vacuum cleaner**
- ☐ **Handheld vacuum cleaner**
- ☐ **Floor mop**
- ☐ **Dust mop**

- ☐ **Angled broom**
- ☐ **Push broom**
- ☐ **Dustpan**
- ☐ **Dusters**
- ☐ **Bucket**
- ☐ **Glass cleaner**
- ☐ **All-purpose cleaner**

- ☐ **Scrub brushes**
- ☐ **Toothbrush** (for tiny corners and grout!)
- ☐ **Counter brush**
- ☐ **Rubber gloves**

the SECRETS of SEWING

Too often, people throw out their perfectly good clothes when a quick fix would make them good as new. If you don't have a designated sewing nook, keep a simple sewing kit in your laundry room. Whatever you do, don't throw your kit into your junk drawers. It needs to be ready at all times!

Putting Together a Sewing Kit

Concentrate on the basics—there's no need for pink thread. Have one spool each of white, black, and "invisible" thread. These three colors will work for most sewing emergencies. It's also good to keep a few different sizes of needles on hand. Make sure to have a selection of buttons, too. Don't forget scissors, a needle threader, and some Velcro strips.

ah, the MEMORIES

"Mom taught us all **HOW TO SEW.** We could pick out the pattern and the fabric and she would pay for it, but we had to **FINISH IT.** This was not a problem at prom or **HOMECOMING**, of course, as we had DEFINITE DEADLINES. If we wanted something from a real **STORE**, we had to buy it ourselves (unless it was on the 60-to-70-percent-off rack)."

— Teresa (No. 5)

Sewing On Replacement Buttons

If you need your dress altered or your suit taken out, it's probably best to drop your clothes off at the tailor unless you really know what you're doing. But anyone—I promise!—can fix a button. Follow these steps.

1

Pull the thread through the eye of the needle until at least twelve inches of thread hangs down each side.

2

From underneath, poke the needle through your shirt where you want the button to be.

3

Place the button on top of the needle. You don't want to attach the button too firmly—place a straight pin between the button and your shirt to avoid this. (You'll pull it out later.)

4

On your first pass, leave a tail of one to two inches. Run the needle through each button's hole, making a crisscross X pattern if there are four holes. This makes for the most secure fastening.

5

To finish off, run the needle through the thread on the underside of the fabric and tie a knot.

SNEAKY SEWING TIPS

Keep these tricks in your back pocket and go from novice to expert in one session flat.

Before starting a job, pull your thread across a candle wick to reduce knotting and tangling.

It's not unusual to nip a shirt when cutting off a loose or broken button. To avoid this, simply slip a comb underneath the button so that the thread goes between the comb's teeth.

In a rush? Try clear nail polish. A quick dab of this stuff will secure and strengthen loose threads. Applying clear nail polish to a stocking run is also the best way to stop it from getting out of control.

Heavier fabrics require thicker thread. If you don't have any, you can always use monofilament fishing line.

Double thread your needle to complete your mend with fewer stitches.

It will be easier to thread your needle if you cut the thread on an angle.

The first place pants wear out is where the heel of your shoe rubs against the inside pant cuff. To avoid wear, sew an extra strip of fabric on the cuff.

ADVENTURES in SEWING

I taught all my girls to sew when they were little. I remember teaching Jane how to make clothes for her dolls from an old pair of socks. And Teresa caught on especially quickly—she was one of the biggest sewers in our house and to this day helps me make curtains and all kinds of things. I sewed all the girls' clothes. Until, that is, they got to be teenagers.

One Sunday, when the boys were out with their dad riding tractors, I thought it would be nice to have some girl sewing time. The girls, I decided, were old enough to make their own clothes. So I let Jane and Teresa rifle through my patterns—from jumpers to blouses to sundresses—to choose what they wanted to make. Teresa picked out a pretty dress with cap sleeves. Jane decided to make a skirt that tied in the front. So far so good. Each girl wrote her measurements on a note card and away we went, piling into the station wagon to head to the fabric store, which was about fifteen miles away. And fifteen miles is a long way when you're listening to: "I want to pick my fabric out first!" and "I don't want you to have the same one as I have!" and "I call pink as my color!" Back and forth, the entire ride.

"You can choose whatever fabric you want," I said as we pulled into the parking lot. We walked into the store and the girls looked around. And then they looked around more. An hour later, I put my foot down. "Teresa, why don't we start looking at some flower prints for you," I said, knowing that she just loved flowers. "I like that one!" she said, pointing at a beautiful fabric with tiny pink, blue, and green blooms. I was impressed with her choice. Jane, however, was not. "I don't want anything that looks like that," she said, and opted instead for a gray, shiny fabric. Done.

When we got home, the girls couldn't wait to get inside. They burst through the front door, took the fabric out of the plastic bags, and had the pieces spread out on the dining table before I walked into the room. Then they started pulling on the cupboard door to get to the sewing machine. "Let me do that," I said. Out came my trusty old Singer. We pulled up three chairs. "I want to go first!" said Jane. "No, I do! I need it sooner than you do," said Teresa. "Hold up," I said. "Let's cut our fabric first."

After we patted down each piece with our hands so there were no wrinkles, I showed them how to place the pattern on the fabric and then carefully cut around it. I took their hands in mine and helped them cut, showing them how to go very slowly and stay on the line.

When we got to the basting step, I explained how basting the fabric helps to avoid puckering and prevents pleats where you're not supposed to have them. "But *you* don't baste when you sew clothes for us," said Teresa. "You just use pins." Kids notice everything! I just told her that the way we were doing it was the better way.

When it got to be time to put the zippers in, boy, was that an event. I didn't want anything to be crooked, so I was strict about doing things over and over until they looked right. "Mom," Teresa said with a frown, "you told me to rip out the zipper three times already! I don't want to try again." "It's almost there," I told her, and then on the next try it was perfect.

CHAPTER 8

a clean
OUTDOORS

I just love being outdoors. I had three gardens at one point, in various spots
around town. Now I have one garden plot in my backyard, and I grow lots
of beautiful flowers, including tulips, irises, daylilies, peonies, and astilbes,
which the girls gave me for Mother's Day. And white lilacs—I adore white
lilac! I love putting my nose in the flowers and just breathing in. The smell
is amazing. But my favorite flower is the lily of the valley. I wanted lilies of
the valley for my bridal bouquet, but the florist said, "You can't afford them!"
I went with red roses instead.

I also grow peppers, spinach, lettuce, cucumbers, radishes, rhubarb, onions, asparagus, and tomatoes in my garden. I once had a strawberry bed too, and I grew lots of beans. When our grandson Jake was small and visiting us, he would say in a very soft, slow voice, "Grandma, how's your garden growing?"

Our outdoor area has changed many times throughout the years. For about twenty years we had an eight-by-twenty-foot cement patio on the south side of our house, and then we built a wood deck in the back of the house. We thought, Great! Now we can sit outside in the morning and on nice evenings. But to our dismay, the mosquitoes put a stop to our enjoyment. To get the best of both worlds—a view of the outdoors and lots of sun but no pests—we decided to build a sunroom over half of the wood deck. We kept costs down by using inexpensive windows—big old windows with no insulation. I was excited to host guests in there, but the first time we had more than six people over it turned out to be too small. If the whole gang came, we'd be walking all over each other. So I asked Vern if he would enclose the entire deck and double our sunroom space. He got right on it. Anything I think of or want, Vern does his darnedest to build it for me. So I've been very fortunate that way.

This time around, we sprung for better-quality, double-paned windows that block UV rays, which can fade your carpeting and upholstery. Now we have a lovely sunroom, where we can eat and watch TV for nine months out of the year. We put in two electric heaters to warm it up in the fall and spring, just while we eat. Vern was very right to install two ceiling fans as well. I call this my eclectic room, because there's all kinds of stuff in here. There are bird figurines everywhere. I say to my grandkids, "Count how many birds are in here. I bet you can't count that high!"

THE GRASS 195
MOWING the LAWN 195
keeping GRASS NATURALLY FERTILIZED 195
WATERING the GRASS 195

the DECK 195
SWEEPING the DECK 195
WASHING DOWN DECK SURFACES 195
WATERING HANGING PLANTS 196
cleaning the LIGHT FIXTURES 196

the PORCH 196
banishing COBWEBS 196
cleaning SCREENS 196
keeping UNWANTED ANIMALS AWAY 196
managing WINDOW BOXES and POTTED PLANTS 197

the GRILL 197
getting a GAS GRILL GREASE-FREE 197
cleaning a CHARCOAL GRILL 197

the FURNITURE 198
cleaning the CUSHIONS 198
washing the UMBRELLA 198
cleaning a HAMMOCK 198
STORING PATIO FURNITURE 198
cleaning OUTDOOR FURNITURE 199

the GARDEN 200

making your GARDEN GROW 200
outsmarting GARDEN SLUGS 200
mastering MULCH 200
getting your VEGETABLES to THRIVE 201
SPRITZING the PLANTS 202
babying BIRDBATHS 202
CURBING CRABGRASS 203

MAKING YOUR OWN COMPOST 204

COMPOST INGREDIENTS 205

MAINTAINING YOUR DRIVEWAY 206

the GARAGE 207

cleaning the GARAGE 207
creating a RECYCLING AREA 207

the CAR 208

eradicating an OIL STAIN 208
washing the CAR 208
cleaning the WINDSHIELDS 208
dealing with a FROZEN LOCK and ICE on the WINDSHIELD 208

CLEANING the GUTTERS 211

TOOLBOX

BRUSHES
Nylon-bristle
Scrub
Soft-bristle
Toothbrush
Vegetable

BUCKETS, GLOVES, and MORE
Bucket
Small garbage pail
Spray bottle
Watering can
Work (or rubber) gloves

CLEANING PRODUCTS
All-purpose cleaning liquid
Baking soda
Detergent
Dishwashing liquid
Rubbing alcohol
White vinegar

CLOTHS, RAGS, SPONGES, and OTHER WIPERS
Chamois cloth
Old sheet or towel
Rags
Sponge
Steel wool
White vinegar

FOR OUTDOORS
Garden trowel
Hose
Mower

SWEEPING, MOPPING, and VACUUMING
Push broom
Vacuum
with attachments

ODOR FIXERS
Active charcoal
Coffee grounds
Fabric softener sheets
Kitty litter
Lemon juice
Oxygen bleach
Vanilla extract

WAXING and POLISHING
Car wax

HANDY to HAVE THESE AROUND
Petroleum jelly
Pipe cleaner
Putty knife
Safety glasses
Shower cap
Tinfoil

the GRASS

Mowing the Lawn

First off, it's important to protect yourself by wearing pants and durable shoes (no flip-flops!). Cut the grass about once a week, when it gets to be two or three inches high. Try to vary your mowing pattern from week to week (horizontal stripes one week, vertical the next) so that you don't compact the soil. Don't cut the grass too short or it'll brown quickly (especially in the summer) and be sure to keep those mower blades high. And if you see that the grass tips are white after you've mowed, that means it's time to have your blades sharpened.

my HOUSE, my RULES

The outside of your house is the **FIRST THING** that guests notice. So do anything you can to make it **TIDY**. I have a hose organizer mounted to the side of my house where we keep our hose. So much **NEATER** than a coil of hose on the ground. Just place it out of **DIRECT SUNLIGHT** or your hose may deteriorate over time.

Keeping Grass Naturally Fertilized

Instead of using purchased fertilizers, just leave your grass clippings on the lawn; they'll decompose and put minerals back into your soil.

Watering the Grass

Give your grass a good sprinkle about twice a week in the evening—half an inch of water each time should do the trick. To see how much you're watering, keep an old coffee can near the sprinkler. Of course, if there's a drought, follow your local watering restrictions.

the DECK

Sweeping the Deck

Insects, leaves, and dirt can get ground in and damage your deck. So use a sturdy outdoor push broom once a week to sweep it off.

Washing Down Deck Surfaces

ALUMINUM: This material is pretty easy to care for. Just give it a good sweep now and then and clean it with soapy water.

TREATED WOOD: Use a putty knife to get any gunk out from between the boards. If you see any mildew, tackle it by scrubbing it with a sponge using a solution of one part oxygen bleach to three parts water. And make sure to shovel snow right after a storm so that the weight of the snow doesn't warp your deck.

COMPOSITE: This mixture of wood and plastic is very low-maintenance. All you need to do is sweep it and wash it down now and then with all-purpose cleaning liquid and water.

Watering Hanging Plants

If you have plants hanging over a porch, patio, or deck, place a shower cap on the undersides of the pots when you water them to catch the drips.

Cleaning the Light Fixtures

Insects tend to gather in these. So take off the glass covers if you can, and rinse them in warm, soapy water. Remove the bulbs and clean them, too, with warm water and dishwashing liquid. If a bulb was tough to remove, smear a bit of petroleum jelly on its thread before you put it back in. You won't have that problem next time. And while you're at it, replace your bulbs with eco-friendly compact fluorescent lightbulbs. They use seventy-five percent less energy than standard incandescent bulbs and last up to ten times longer. It's money in the bank and good for the planet, too!

the PORCH

Banishing Cobwebs

Don't let dust and cobwebs intrude on your outdoor relaxation. Use a push broom once a week to sweep them away.

Cleaning Screens

Porch screens can get filled with dust and pollen. Remove the screens when they start looking dusty and bring them outside. Wet a scrub brush with hot, soapy water, scrub the screens, and rinse them down with a hose.

Keeping Unwanted Animals Away

Stray cats and other animals will sometimes find their way onto your porch. This can be a nuisance (especially if they like to munch on your plants or mark their territory). Wash down your porch with diluted white vinegar and rinse it with the hose. Cats hate the smell of vinegar.

ah, the MEMORIES

"Exercise was big in our house—we were a very **ATHLETIC** family, and a **COMPETITIVE** one too. There was always a game going on out back. Mom's thing was 'We've got to **KEEP THESE KIDS BUSY**.' She felt that it was the way to build **HEALTHY MINDS** and to teach us how to fend for ourselves. She always said 'When you go out in the world, your corners will be rounded off.'"

— Tom (No. 1)

Managing Window Boxes and Potted Plants

Your plants will thrive with the proper drainage system. Place a layer of broken crockery or pebbles at the bottom of the boxes or pots to help them out. It's also easy to make your own potting soil: equal parts mature compost (see page 204), garden soil, and sand.

the GRILL

Getting a Gas Grill Grease-Free

When all the burgers have been eaten, close the lid and turn the heat on high for about fifteen minutes to cook off excess food. Let the grill cool completely, then roll some tinfoil into a ball and use it to scrub the grates and burners. Use a pipe cleaner to get food remnants out of any holes. To clean the exterior, wipe it down with dishwashing liquid and water and rinse well—who wants soapy-smelling hot dogs? About once a year, get built-up grease off those grates by applying a solution of equal parts white vinegar and water. Let it sit for about an hour before scraping away. Grilling to me is a social thing; you talk to the person who is grilling, you have a bottle of beer, and it's terrific for when the kids come over.

Cleaning a Charcoal Grill

Use a plastic putty knife to remove grease and grime. Then use steel wool, hot water, and mild dishwashing liquid to clean it all up. Vinegar is great for getting out grease stains, too. To make your charcoal grill last season after season, sprinkle half an inch of sand at the bottom of the canister to catch hot grease. Vern made our first charcoal grill out of an old hot-water heater. It was really big— nice because you could make a lot of hamburgers on it, but it was just too large for my taste.

WASTE NOT WANT NOT

Try to reuse water whenever possible. When I'm changing the water in the fish tank, I put the old water in a pan and use it on my plants—it's great for fertilizing. And I save the water from washing my tights and use it on my plants too; same goes for the water left over from boiling potatoes, pasta, or eggs (just be sure to let it cool first). If that bottle of club soda went flat, you can use that, too—the minerals make plants very happy. And keep a barrel under your gutters to collect rainwater.

the FURNITURE

Cleaning the Cushions

Most outdoor cushions are stain-resistant, so you won't need to use too much muscle. Just use a scrub brush and some mild soap (harsher detergents can take off the protective coating). Let the cushions dry thoroughly so mold doesn't form, and place them in a storage chest before you go to bed every night, just in case it rains.

Washing the Umbrella

Use the hose to rinse your umbrella every few weeks or whenever it looks dirty. For heavier cleaning, or to tackle tough mildew, the fabric part of many umbrellas (check labels) can be removed and placed in the washing machine with cold water and mild detergent. Don't put it in the dryer, though. Reattach it to the frame and keep it open to dry.

Cleaning a Hammock

Lay it flat on an old sheet and clean it with a nylon scrub brush dipped in warm water and all-purpose cleaning liquid. Then flip it over and repeat on the other side. Rinse with a hose and hang it on the line to dry.

Storing Patio Furniture

When the season ends, thoroughly clean and dry the furniture, then bring the pillows and the umbrellas into either the basement or garage. As for the chairs and tables, if you have space, store them, otherwise cover them with heavy-duty patio covers. Tie the covers onto the furniture so they won't blow away in high winds.

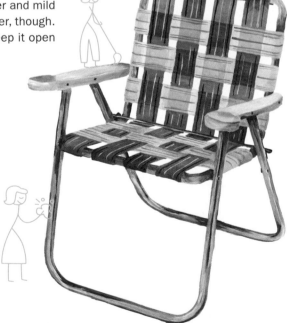

CLEANING OUTDOOR FURNITURE

Here's how to care for the most common materials.

MATERIAL	METHOD
ALUMINUM	Wash with warm water and mild dishwashing liquid. Some sunscreens (especially those containing PABA) can stain aluminum, so place a towel over the chair before sitting if you've just lubed up.
IRON AND STEEL	These materials tend to rust when exposed to the elements. So check periodically for rust, and if you see any, gently buff it with steel wool.
PLASTIC	This isn't the most durable option, so it's good to give it a little extra protection. I like to wipe car wax on plastic to prevent stains. For regular cleaning, apply a solution of water and dishwashing liquid with a soft-bristle brush.
TEAK	This naturally rot- and water-resistant wood rarely needs to be cleaned and can actually be left outside all year long—it'll develop a beautiful silver patina over time. Clean with dishwashing liquid and water using a soft brush.
AND OTHER WOOD	Clean with dishwashing liquid and water.
WICKER	Whether your wicker furniture is made of plant fibers, resin, or vinyl, you'll want to flip it over to dislodge dirt from those crevices. Then vacuum the textured surface. To get into the tight crevices, use an old toothbrush and scrub with dishwashing liquid and water. Wipe the piece down, then place it in the sun to dry. Natural wicker may wear away over time if kept in direct sun; a shady spot is best.

the GARDEN

Making Your Garden Grow

I've learned a few tricks about gardening in my day. I'll share them with you:

✳ You'll want to water about an inch a week; never overwater—that's just the worst for plants. And water the base of the plant rather than the leaves, or fungus will form. Let the hose run slowly, so that the water has time to seep in and doesn't run off— that's just a waste of water. I put the kitchen timer on for twenty minutes to remind me to move the hose from plant to plant.

✳ Sprinkle coffee grounds in and around your plants once a week to enrich the soil.

✳ When creating garden beds, sift your topsoil through an old window screen. No chunks. Our black Iowa soil is so mellow, we didn't need to bother with this trick, but it's a good one if your soil has clumps.

Outsmarting Garden Slugs

Slugs are often bad news, wreaking havoc on your newly planted garden. The best way to deal with them is to place pieces of cardboard on the bare soil around your plantings in the late afternoon. The next morning, turn over the boards, scrape the slugs into a plastic container, and place it in the freezer for three hours. Once the slugs are frozen you can dump them onto your compost pile.

Mastering Mulch

Mulching your garden is key: It keeps the soil warm (plants grow faster that way), water in the ground (meaning less watering for you), and weeds at bay. Black garbage bags are great for container tomato gardens, because they warm the soil (tomatoes will love this). Or you can plant tomatoes in your yard and mulch them with leaves (it's best to chop the leaves up first), straw, or wood chips left over from around-the-house projects.

ah, the MEMORIES

"When many of us were home in the summer and eating the **EVENING MEAL** together and our phone would ring during the dinner hour, Mom would answer the phone '**MEYER'S SUMMER HOME.** Some are home and some are not!' and then take a MESSAGE and return to the meal."
— Jane (No. 6)

GETTING YOUR VEGETABLES to THRIVE

I love growing my own food for two reasons: You know there are no pesticides on it, and kids are more apt to eat their veggies when they helped to grow them. I've learned to plant marigolds among beans, spinach, and tomatoes; the flowers have a chemical in them that kills the insects that can ruin these goodies. Here are some other tips.

RADISHES	When it comes to radishes, I follow the *Farmer's Almanac*. It says that you have to plant them by the dark of the moon or they'll go to tops. The only thing I follow the *Farmer's Almanac* for is my radishes. The years I don't follow it, I don't have radishes.
RHUBARB	Every year, I make rhubarb crisp with raspberry jam. But rhubarb leaves are poisonous, so you have to make sure your kids and pets don't eat them. Now and then I'll get down low and pull up the leaves, because they're great for mulching. You can also use them to make a solution to keep aphids away. Put about a pound of chopped rhubarb leaves in a pot and pour two pints of boiling water over them; let the mixture sit overnight, strain it, and then add a tablespoon of detergent. Place the liquid in a spray bottle and spritz your plants with it every now and then.
PARSLEY	My parsley plants came up this year from seeds planted ages ago. I was so tickled.
ONIONS	I grow them every year, and since they're hardy perennials, I keep them going and don't even have to do anything. They just come up! I like to plant them next to my beets and carrots, because they keep bugs away.
CUCUMBERS	I try to keep cucumbers mulched with rhubarb leaves or grass clippings to prevent weeds and rotting.
TOMATOES and PEPPERS	Water these about an inch a week, and watch them grow like the dickens!

Spritzing the Plants

Once in a while it's a good idea to spray the leaves of your plants to prevent pests. If you hand-wash your dishes, save the left-over soapy water and put it in a spray bottle —soap is great for killing pests like mites.

Babying Birdbaths

Whether you have stone or terra-cotta birdbaths, they get moldy pretty quick. So scrub them out with water and a vegetable brush. Birds like their baths clean—otherwise, they won't take a dip.

ah, the MEMORIES

"We spent a lot of time **OUTSIDE**—playing, doing chores, even eating dinner. We had so many dinners around that picnic table. If it was **WARM** we'd be out there. In fact, even if it **WASN'T THAT WARM**, we'd be out there. A lot of my memories from around the **PICNIC TABLE** have us in jackets and sweaters."

— Joe (No. 7)

CURBING CRABGRASS

Crabgrass is one of the most common grass weeds. If you have some, you probably know that it is almost impossible to eliminate entirely. Here are a few steps you can take to prevent crabgrass from completely ruining your lawn.

A thick, healthy lawn will act as its own protection, as crabgrass can't take root without sunlight reaching the soil. Keeping your grass at about two and a half or three inches high limits the amount of light that gets down there.

Pull out crabgrass as soon as you see it. A small patch can quickly turn into a full-blown problem.

Make sure you get the entire root. Pliers can be really helpful for this. Crabgrass is a sturdy weed and will grow wherever its roots touch.

MAKING YOUR OWN COMPOST

Why buy compost for your garden when you can make it yourself? It's so much cheaper that way, and if you start now it'll be ready in about two months.

Look around your yard for an out-of-the-way (but not too far, or else you'll dread going), partly sunny, partly shady spot.

You can use a wooden or metal bin—four-foot-by-eight-feet is fine, though you can go smaller if you don't have the space— a hole the ground is fine, too.

Line the bottom with a bunch of twigs, then gather carbon-rich "browns" (anything from chopped-up dried leaves and branches to straw), and nitrogen-rich "greens" (grass clippings and kitchen waste, from eggshells and tea bags to banana peels, but no meat or dairy products or you'll attract pests).

Be sure to build a compost that is pest-proof, especially if you are a city dweller.

Ideally, your compost pile should have one part green materials to two parts brown ones, so that everything breaks down correctly.

When you start a pile you'll need to follow these layering instructions, but after that you can just add things to the pile. Put six to eight inches of your organic (brown) matter down, followed by a thin layer of garden soil (or horse manure, if you have that sort of thing). Repeat these layers three times. Then turn your pile every other week with a rake.

Keep your greens in a sealed container in your freezer, and take them out to the compost pile once a week. Remember to thaw them first.

The compost should be moist, so water it whenever it's looking dry. You'll know it's ready to go when it's brown, crumbles freely, and smells deliciously earthy.

I keep a nice rustic table next to my compost bin for filling up my pots with a soil-and-compost mixture.

COMPOST INGREDIENTS

GREENS	fruit and vegetable scraps coffee grounds and filters household plant trimmings	soft prunings eggshells tea bags	grass clippings flowers hair
BROWNS	twigs and branches mulch from rain gutters shredded newspaper paper egg cartons	fallen leaves pine needles wood ashes wood chips	sawdust dryer lint straw
THINGS to AVOID	anything treated with pesticides or herbicides animal and dairy products oil and grease	diseased or poisonous plants weeds and any plants that aren't completely dead (they can take root in your compost pile, which you don't want)	

Traditional trash bags can take decades and even centuries to decompose (there is some debate on the actual number of years). Luckily, there are some new products on the market that decompose much faster than traditional bags. Look for bags made of corn-based materials.

MAINTAINING YOUR DRIVEWAY

Taking good care of your driveway will save you a fortune in repairs. Follow this guide to maintaining the most common types.

TYPE	MAINTENANCE
ASPHALT	Over the years, an asphalt driveway will develop small cracks. These cracks can be repaired with blacktop crack filler and a caulking gun.
CONCRETE	Parked cars drip oil and can quickly stain a concrete driveway. A shallow pan filled with sand or sawdust placed under your car will catch the drips.
GRAVEL	A quick rake of a gravel driveway every so often will even out the surface and hide oil stains.
STONE OR BRICK	A driveway made of one of these materials requires more attention, because moss and mildew love them. Mildew can be scrubbed away using a mixture of water and chlorine. Moss should be removed, too, as wet moss can be very slippery. Garden lime works well on moss, but make sure you wear gloves and a mask when handling it. After sprinkling the lime liberally on the moss, allow a few days for it to dry up and then sweep it away.

the GARAGE

Cleaning the Garage

Back the cars out and sweep the garage once a week with a sturdy push broom. Some suggest spritzing the floor with water first, because that'll keep the dust and dirt from swirling around your face as you work. I've never tried, though it seems like a fine idea. One of the best things you can do to keep the garage from turning into a big old mess is to create different zones for different things. If your family is as big on athletics as mine was, put all of the sports gear, from baseball bats to skis to soccer balls, in one area. Arrange storage bins by sport, so kids can go right up to the baseball bin to find their bats and balls. This makes putting things away easier, because they'll only have to return stuff to one area. Likewise, if you're an avid gardener like I am, you can set up a potting station here and keep all of your soil, pots, and tools in one place. Think about items that can be stored on pegs and hooks, like tennis racquets, nets, and bikes, to keep the floors and shelves less cluttered.

Creating a Recycling Area

Make life easy on yourself by placing two big plastic bins near the door to your garage: one for cans and bottles, one for paper. Collect your recycled paper from around the house daily and deposit it into your paper bin. Wash cans and bottles out and recycle them right away.

my **HOUSE,** my **RULES**

Now, the garage and the cars are typically **VERN'S** territory, but I've picked up some know-how along the way. And let me tell you, we spent a lot of time in the **CAR**. That station wagon was always on the move. And in the summers, we'd take trips **NEAR AND FAR** in our MOTOR HOME. One thing, though: When you have nine kids, you really have to keep an eye on them. One time, as we left a filling station during a trip through Kansas in our motor home, Vern saw **TWO CHILDREN** running to catch up with us and wondered who they were. I **COUNTED HEADS**, and sure enough, they were ours: **MARIA** and **PAT**.

the CAR

Eradicating an Oil Stain

Sop up all the oil on the garage floor by sprinkling some kitty litter on the spot and moving it around a bit with a wooden spoon. Let it sit for about ten minutes, then pour just enough boiling water to cover the area. Use a stiff broom or scrub brush to scour the area before rinsing with cool water. When you're done, sprinkle some baking soda on top. Should do the trick.

Washing the Car

First, vacuum the interior. We had to vacuum the maroon station wagon weekly, but most people can get by vacuuming once a month or so. Then, for the exterior: Fill a bucket with all-purpose liquid soap and warm water, then clean the car with a big, soft sponge, paying attention to the tires, too. Dry it with an old towel, and then make it shine by rubbing the surface with a chamois cloth.

Cleaning the Windshields

Rubbing alcohol is great for getting grime, like what that bird left behind, off your windshield (just don't get any rubbing alcohol on the paint). Apply it with a soft cloth. And don't forget to clean the wiper blades, too, so they stop leaving those annoying smear marks. Use a cloth dipped in diluted detergent—great for swiping away those dead bugs.

Dealing with a Frozen Lock and Ice on the Windshield

If the lock on your car or trunk door has frozen up, light a match and heat the key for a few seconds. Put it in the cylinder and the ice should melt fast. Use hot water to melt the ice on the windshield. A hairdryer will also work.

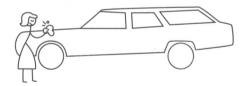

ah, the MEMORIES

"My dad would **TRAVEL** now and then for his job at John Deere. And I always remember that Mom instructed him to bring home **SOAP** from the various motels and hotels he stayed at. Dad always said that she knew how to make a **BUFFALO NICKEL SQUEAL**."

— Tim (No. 2)

FAMILY VACATION:
THE MOTOR HOME

"Dad was a farm boy from Kansas, and he could build anything. In the summer of 1964, Mom and Dad had eight kids, and Dad was just about to finish building us a motor home so we could take trips to places like Billings, Montana, and the Rio Grande Valley. Mom said to him, 'Can you build it for nine?' That was her way of telling my dad that I was on the way. I remember sleeping in the back of the motor home with my brothers. We all slept in there like puppies."

— Dan (No. 9)

"When we traveled with Mom and Dad in our motor home, Mom always got out at the place where we stopped to pay and would go walk to find the site to park. We never understood why Dad took his time paying, but now I realize that it was probably the only time Mom could have to herself. Dad would drive around the park until he found her, and Mom would have already found a spot with no one else around."

— Jane (No. 6)

"Mom always instilled in us the notion that life was an adventure. Every summer we went on vacation to see the world (or at least as far as our cousin's farm in Kansas), and we went on many other trips in the motor home as well. My favorite trip was when Mom and Dad took us down the Green River in Utah for a weeklong river-rafting vacation. I never sensed that Mom and Dad were worried about how I or any of us would do when we went off to college; it was like it was expected that we'd do fine, that we'd had enough life experiences up to that point that we'd be able to handle things on our own. That's not to say we couldn't call home for advice, but we knew we should try to figure it out on our own first."

— Maria (No. 4)

Get yourself a sturdy LADDER and a pair of NONSLIP shoes.

CLEANING the GUTTERS

If gutters are going to do their job, they have to be clear of debris and leaves, otherwise drain outlets will dam up, overflow, and pull gutters loose. To save yourself time and money repairing your gutters, clean them out twice a year. This isn't for folks afraid of heights or unsteady on their feet!

Get yourself a sturdy ladder and a pair of nonslip shoes. Only clean the gutters on nice days (never in icy or wet weather!). Wear your work gloves too, and some safety glasses, and bring a small garbage pail or plastic bag with you.

1

REMOVE LOOSE LEAVES and DEBRIS

Start at the drain outlet at the low end of a gutter. Take a narrow garden trowel and scoop that debris into a garbage can. It's usually easiest to do this when the debris is slightly damp and pliable, not dried and crinkly.

2

BLAST THOSE GUTTERS

Using your hose's spray nozzle, wash out each length of gutter, working toward the drain outlet. This can quickly turn into a mess if you're not careful, ending with your splattering mud all over the house. So watch what you're doing! You can use a stiff scrub brush to break loose encrusted dirt if you get it on the house.

3

CLEAR OBSTRUCTIONS in DRAINPIPES

If water doesn't drain freely through the drainpipes, try flushing debris down them with the hose. If that doesn't work, use a snake to free and pull out gunk from the bottom.

LOVE thy NEIGHBOR

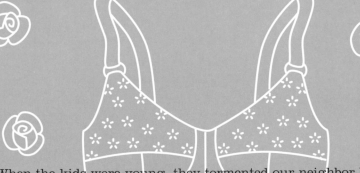

When the kids were young, they tormented our neighbor Elsie, who is now ninety-three and still next door. In fact, she became a grand neighbor after the kids left. Elsie and her husband didn't have children of their own, and living next door to a family with nine kids couldn't have been easy.

Elsie believed in keeping order. She was spic-and-span, all right. She had the most beautiful garden that she tended to every day, and let me tell you, you wouldn't want to be a weed in Elsie's garden. But she did learn one lesson from my kids: Don't wear your unmentionables when you tend to the tomatoes. One day, Tom and Tim ran to me screaming "Hey, Mom, come look! Elsie's outside in her bra!" Now, there was no way she didn't hear their screeching. They would go upstairs into our family room and look down into her backyard from the east window, and many times she'd be out there in just her bra. Geez.

Another hot summer day, I was painting the garden shed with Tom and Tim. We'd decided on a beautiful, rustic gray. They must have been about eleven years old at the time. It was so humid that they were wearing just their shorts, and I had on my painting clothes. I brought out some buckets of water for us to clean our brushes in, and right away Tom swished his brush in the water and slapped it right against Elsie's redwood fence. Paint splattered everywhere. For a second I hoped that maybe she just wouldn't notice. But oh, no. Elsie notices everything. She got up from her kneeling position by the zucchinis she was pulling up and made a beeline for Tom. "What do you think you're doing?" she screamed. "Do you realize you're going to have to paint my entire fence gray now?!" She had such a fit.

One night I went out walking and saw that there were beer cans all over Elsie's yard. You see, the neighborhood kids knew she was easily upset, so they weren't very nice to her. Sometimes they'd knock on her door and then run away. And other times, like this night, they'd toss beer cans on her lawn. Sometimes they'd even drink in her yard, if they were feeling particularly naughty. Well, I wasn't feeling naughty that night. "I'm going to pick up these cans for Elsie," I said to myself. "She needs a break now and then just like everyone else." So that's just what I did. I went inside, grabbed a plastic sack, stuffed every can inside, and put the sack in our yard. Well, I must not have knotted the sack very tightly, because come morning, all those cans had blown right back onto Elsie's front yard. When Vern went to work he saw the wind-blown cans. As he was picking them up, Elsie screamed "Vern! Do you know what your wife does during the night?!" Oh, that Elsie—she thought I was carousing around town.

PETS,

ODORS,

and PESTS

It takes more than animal instinct to care for pets—and the odors they inevitably leave behind. Insects, too, need to be dealt with—and fast. Arm yourself with the following know-how.

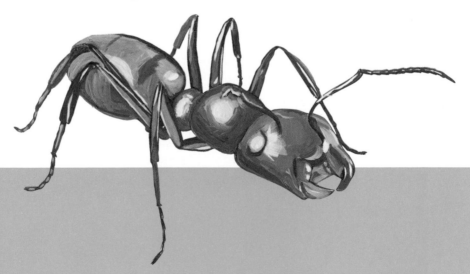

PET CARE

Animals were big in our house. We always had a new critter coming or going because there's something special about kids growing up with animals. I think it's a great opportunity to not only teach children responsibility, but also for them to give and receive extra affection. But taking care of them can be a beast if you're not prepared. Here are some of my tips for keeping your furry friends wagging and purring all day long.

Brushing Fluffy And Fido

Pets love the sensation of being brushed, and you'll benefit from the act too, because less hair will end up on your sofa. For cats, a regular brushing means fewer hairballs. So do this—outdoors if you can—about once a week. To control odors, sprinkle some baking soda on your pet before brushing.

Fighting Off Fleas

To stop fleas from coming around in the first place, squirt a few drops of orange oil in your pet's shampoo. Or add some brewer's yeast or garlic to his food (when he's not looking, of course). If your pet already has fleas, brush him with a flea comb and vacuum his sleeping area thoroughly to suck up fleas and their eggs (toss the vacuum cleaner's bag immediately afterward). There are a few things that you can place near your pet's sleeping quarters to repel fleas: cedar shavings, pine needles, eucalyptus oil, and saltwater (sprinkle salt in water and clean the area).

Keeping the Cat Away from Plants

Anytime your precious kitty goes near your greenery—or anywhere you don't want him to, for that matter—either spray him with water or dab a little white vinegar on his mouth with a cotton ball. He'll soon learn to stay far from your fern if he knows he'll be getting a taste of that vinegar, that's for sure. If your cat tends to bat around the soil in your potted plants, place some balled-up pantyhose on top of the soil; you can pour water right onto the nylon.

Stopping Scratching

I can't tell you how many times I used to come into the living room to find another scratch on a chair or ottoman. Drove me nuts! So it's important to provide a scratching post. You can create a makeshift one by wrapping a spare piece of carpet around some wood.

Changing the Litter

Wear rubber gloves when dealing with the litter box to cut down on germ transfer. For easier cleaning, line the box with newspaper, and sprinkle some baking soda on top before adding the litter to absorb odors. Clean the box once a week with dishwashing liquid and warm water, then put it outside for half an hour to air it out.

Washing the Dog

So that you don't get soaked, make yourself a smock by cutting two armholes and a hole for your head out of a plastic garbage bag, and put it on. If it's warm enough, take the dog outside, and try to get him to stand in a large bin or a child's pool while you hose him off so that his feet can get a good soak while you're at it.

Bathing Your Cat

The best way to keep pet allergies under control is to give your pet regular baths. Now, if you've ever tried bathing your cat, you know how much he hates it, but if you start right when he is a kitten, he'll get used to it. If it's too late for that, try baby wipes. Since cats clean themselves, once a month should be plenty often.

Getting out Urine Stains

Cat urine is the worst—it contains a chemical that can permanently discolor a carpet or floor. And don't even get me started on the smell. It's one of those terribly tough smells to get out, and a little cat urine can, in some cases, mean having to throw out a rug or a piece of furniture. But here's something you can try: Blot as much as you can with a rag. Then, using a new rag, apply a solution of a quarter teaspoon of dishwashing liquid to one cup of warm water. Blot again, rinse, and blot once more. Then apply a mixture of one part white vinegar to two parts water; blot until dry.

Maintaining the Hamster/Gerbil/Guinea-Pig Cage

Keep your little guy in a glass terrarium instead of a cage and you won't have to deal with litter sneaking through the sides and the bottom. (And don't use a cardboard box. He can gnaw through it.) In addition to his regular food, toss in some raw carrots now and then to satisfy his need to chew. And place the food in a ceramic or metal bowl instead of a plastic one; these critters can chew through plastic in no time. We had many hamsters over the years, and they're pretty low-maintenance.

DEALING with a
SKUNK ATTACK

Immediately give your pet a TOMATO-JUICE bath and let him soak in there for as long as he can stand it. Follow up with a SHAMPOO bath.

GENERAL PET-IQUETTE

Everybody wants to have as relaxed a household as possible, which means a lot of you are going to get your dander up when I say no pets on the furniture. Although pets are of course members of your family, they're not people.

Do not let pets sleep in bed with you or your children. Among other things, pets can interrupt a good night's sleep.

Don't let pets on your furniture.
Train your pets to keep to the floor.
Keep them off your counters, too.

Don't feed pets uncooked food.
Is Snoofers drooling at that raw steak? Don't even give him a bite: Pets can get food-borne illnesses just like humans.

Keep your pet dishes clean, just as you would your own!
Wash food and water bowls in hot, soapy water
before you refill them.

Be sure to always rinse pet dishes thoroughly. The taste of soap might upset your pet's appetite, or even make him sick.

SMELL PATROL

Does something stink? Sniff out the situation and get cracking.

KITCHEN ODORS		Whether it's last night's fish lingering or the garbage that someone was supposed to take out but didn't, a bad odor can be curbed with a citrus scent. Pour some lemon juice and water into a spray bottle and spritz the room with it. Or you can boil white vinegar in a pan on the stove and place a fabric-softener sheet at the bottom of your garbage can. And open the windows for an hour or so to air the place out.
BATHROOM ODORS		Light a match! And keep a scented candle nearby at all times.
SNEAKER ODORS		Stuff some newspaper in there; it'll absorb moisture.

CIGARETTE ODORS		Citrus scents work wonders to mask this harsh smell. But the best thing to do is not smoke in the first place. It's very bad for you. I never allowed it—not from anyone—in my home or my cars.
BASEMENT ODORS		Trapped moisture is the reason old books, comforters, and suitcases can take on a musty smell. Place the items in a container with a baggie filled with active charcoal, which will absorb the stench in a day or so.
FRIDGE ODORS		To combat odors from week-old leftovers, pour some vanilla extract onto a cotton ball and place it on a dish in the fridge for a few days. And keep baking soda in there, always. It's a good standby.
HAND ODORS		When you've been slicing garlic or an onion, sometimes it can be difficult to rid your hands of the smell. Either rub them with fresh lemon or dampen them with water and rub them on a stainless-steel faucet—it works!

PESTS

It's important to make your home undesirable to these critters in the first place. Clean up spills right away, keep a lid on the trash and take it out every day, and place dry goods like cereal and sugar in airtight containers. Now, if you do come across a creepy-crawly, there are natural, nontoxic ways to prevent it from ever coming back.

Annihilating Ants

Try to figure out where the ants are coming from, then sprinkle chili powder near the source; ants tend not to cross a chili-powder path. Same goes for slices of cucumber, mint leaves, coffee grounds, or clove: they'll steer clear of them, too. You can also squirt them with hot, soapy water from a spray bottle. If you need a stronger solution, try this: Mix a teaspoon of boric acid crystals (which should be kept away from kids and pets) with two and a half ounces of corn syrup. Heat the mixture on the stove until the crystals dissolve. Let it cool, then add an equal amount of water. Use this in your spray bottle and spritz away.

Revolting against Roaches

Roaches are drawn to water, so fix leaky faucets as soon as you can, and never leave standing water in your bathroom or kitchen sink. Roaches also love wallpaper paste, so make sure to fix any rips fast. To get them good, either leave small bowls filled with hot, soapy water around the house or fill a spray bottle with the stuff and squirt offenders whenever you see them; this will usually kill them quickly. You can also put catnip wherever you see roaches; they'll run from it. Or consider placing cucumber peels in moist areas like sinks and tubs, and dried bay leaves in your cupboards. If those don't work, create this mixture (which will also deter ants): one cup of borax, a quarter cup of crushed red pepper, and a quarter cup of crushed bay leaves. Pour in a bowl and place the bowl in your pantry.

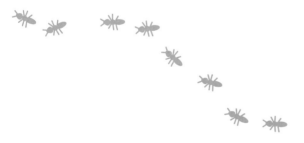

Outsmarting Mice

So a mouse has started to call your kitchen countertop home. Want to know how to trap the squeaker without killing it? Put a piece of cheese at one end of a paper-towel tube. Position the tube so that half of it hangs off the counter (with the cheese at that end). Place a large cardboard box on the floor underneath your contraption. The mouse will smell the cheese and run into the tube to get it. Its weight will cause the tube to tip, making it (and the mouse) fall into the box. Caught red-handed. Other things to do: Get metal trash cans (rodents can chew through plastic ones), make sure you have tight-fitting lids for them, and keep them raised at least a foot off the floor, so that, hopefully, rodents will just walk on by.

Killing Kitchen Bugs

Many times you'll get little bugs coming home with you in your bags of grain or flour. If you see some, place the bags in the freezer for a few days to kill the bugs.

Fighting Off Flies

Nothing's more annoying than a fly buzzing around your head. Spray the little bugger with hairspray to slow it down. Then you'll be able to get it with a flyswatter. To keep flies from returning, plant basil outside your front and back doors. They don't like basil all that much.

Sending Spiders on Their Way

Sure, we all love *Charlotte's Web*. But you don't necessarily want a spider in your living room. To ward off spiders, wipe the insides and outsides of your windows with rubbing alcohol, and place cotton balls soaked in rubbing alcohol near entryways.

GLOSSARY
of SELECTED TERMS

All cleaning supplies can be found at
GROCERY, HOME, OR **HARDWARE**
stores unless otherwise noted.

DUSTING, WIPING, and SCRUBBING

BRUSHES

COUNTER A speedy and scratch-free tool for removing dust and dirt from highly polished surfaces. A good choice for granite, marble, stainless steel, and wood. Look for fine nylon or natural bristles.

PAINTBRUSH Use it on fragile items like lamp shades, things with intricate designs, or to reach tight spaces. Keep paintbrushes for dusting separate from those for paint touch-ups.

SCRUB A brush with bristles inserted into a rectangular block. Use it for scrubbing floors and walls.

SOFT-BRISTLE Good for cleaning glassware, antiques, and most household surfaces.

STIFF-BRISTLE A stiff nylon-bristle brush is ideal for thoroughly scrubbing surfaces with crevices and textures. The handle will help keep your knuckles from getting scraped.

TOILET Needed for scrubbing the inside of the toilet bowl. Nylon bristles work best.

TOOTHBRUSH Old toothbrushes can be used to clean hard-to-reach spots in the kitchen, bath, and other places around the house. Use them to remove grime from faucets, light switches, cabinet hardware, and jewelry.

CLOTHS

CHAMOIS A soft suede-textured material that is lint-free and can absorb a good amount of water. Natural chamois is made from animal skin. Imitation chamois is made of cotton or synthetic fibers and is much less expensive. Chamois is good for wiping down large surfaces, such as lawn furniture or cars, as well as delicate surfaces that may scratch. Rinse and wring chamois well before use.

DUST A good dust cloth should attract and capture dust. Look for a soft cotton such as flannel.

LINT-FREE Use these thin, woven towels for wiping mirrors and any other surfaces. Flour-sack and huck towels, cloth diapers, and cut-up old white cotton T-shirts make excellent lint-free cloths.

MICROFIBER Woven from superfine synthetic fibers, the surface of the cloth is designed to trap dirt. Use it on surfaces prone to scratching, such as acrylic and stainless-steel appliances.

MUSLIN A finely-woven unbleached or white cotton cloth. Use for dusting artwork or lining cedar chests so that clothes don't come into contact with wood.

POLISHING Soft, napped cloths that are used to polish and buff silver or other metals. Choose untreated, 100 percent cotton flannel, which is softer than plain cotton.

CLEANING PRODUCTS

ALL-PURPOSE CLEANING LIQUID Great on all nonporous surfaces such as finished wood and tile floors, countertops, walls, porcelain, bathroom fixtures, and sealed natural and synthetic stone.

BABY WIPES These towelettes are premoistened with a baby-safe wash and are just the right size for a variety of other household cleanups. Use them to take makeup, crayon, and even heel marks from floors, tiles, and walls.

BAKING SODA Its mild abrasive action and natural deodorizing properties make it a great replacement for harsh scouring powders. Use it as a cleaner, deodorizer, and stain remover.

BORAX Borax is a naturally occurring mineral that has water-softening and whitening properties. Use it as a laundry booster (especially when washing cloth diapers) and to clean and deodorize.

CARPET CLEANER Many commercial carpet cleaners contain harsh chemicals. Look for nontoxic options or make your own spot cleaner (a quarter teaspoon of dishwashing liquid diluted in a quart of water) to extend a carpet's life.

COUNTERTOP SPRAY (also called surface spray) A cleanser that works well on all nonporous surfaces such as finished wood, tiled floors, countertops, walls, and sealed granite and marble.

DISHWASHING LIQUID Designed to keep dishes clean and bright, this cleanser cuts grease and is mild enough to use for many other household cleaning tasks.

OXYGEN BLEACH Available as both liquids and powders, these bleaches are gentler and less toxic than chlorine bleach. Oxygen bleaches maintain colors and help keep whites white (but will not make them whiter). They are safe to use on colored cotton, wool, silk, and synthetic fabrics. Add to the wash at the same time you add the detergent. Most effective with hot water.

SOLVENT CLEANER Solvents work to dissolve oil-based stains like grease and tar. Be very careful when handling or disposing.

WINDOW-CLEANING LIQUID To help keep windows, mirrors, and glass sparkling and streak-free.

CLUB SODA Carbonated water can help remove stains from fabrics and carpets, and clean glass and countertops.

COLA The acid in a can of cola may remove stains from a toilet bowl.

COMPRESSED AIR Great for cleaning keyboards, piano keys, and other hard-to-reach spots that can't tolerate moisture. Buy this in office-supply stores.

CREAM OF TARTAR Cream of tartar, a natural acid salt, is a byproduct of wine making and can be used to clear discoloration from aluminum and copper pots and pans and silverware. It can also get rid of stains on porcelain.

DENTURE TABLETS They have a bleaching compound that helps whiten and disinfect dentures, and they'll do the same job on many other things around your household, such as toilets and sinks.

DISTILLED WATER Water purified to eliminate any minerals, chemicals, or trace elements. Cleans electronics and delicate metals and antiques without mineral buildup.

DRYER SHEETS Dryer sheets are soft and designed to reduce static but can also remove dust from window blinds or electrical appliances such as televisions and computer screens. They also keep closets fresh.

DRY SPONGE Ideal for cleaning surfaces that can be damaged by moisture. Use it completely dry as you would a rubber eraser, to absorb dirt and gently clean papered or porous walls.

DUSTERS

EXTENDABLE This long-handled tool is essential for high and hard-to-reach places such as ceiling fans and skylights.

FEATHER Perfect for small crevices or to to sweep across large surfaces. Use it for general dusting, on end tables, bookshelves, lamps, and more.

HYDROGEN PEROXIDE A chemical that works as a disinfectant and bleaching agent. Because this chemical is essentially water with an extra oxygen molecule, it is kinder on the environment than chlorine bleach. Use it as a bathroom disinfectant and cleaner or to spot-clean many fabrics.

KETCHUP The acids in ketchup can help make tarnished copper pots and pans gleam.

NEWSPAPER Give your old newspapers extra life by using them to clean windows and mirrors.

OLIVE OIL Use it to clean pearls and polish lacquered metal.

PADS

NYLON SCRUBBY Good for keeping most household surfaces scratch-free.

STEEL WOOL Because this super-abrasive pad can scratch most surfaces, it should only be used to scrub the most stubborn stains.

POULTICE A non-acidic, absorbent cleaning powder that can be made from common house-hold ingredients or purchased from hardware or tile stores. Poultices are formulated to remove deep-set stains without ruining a surface.

PUMICE STONE This hard stone is great for scrubbing off stains from hard surfaces.

RUBBING ALCOHOL Use it to polish chrome and windows; disinfect phones, doorknobs, and the exterior of appliances; and remove fresh ink or marker stains from fabrics and carpets.

TABASCO SAUCE This hot sauce, made from peppers, vinegar, and salt, contains acid that helps remove tarnish from brass.

TOOTHPASTE A mild abrasive, toothpaste contains ingredients such as baking soda and hydrogen peroxide. Use it to polish chrome and dull-looking jewelry and remove stains on walls and carpets.

WASHING SODA Washing soda (sodium carbonate decahydrate) is a mineral that cuts grease; cleans walls, tiles, sinks, and tubs; and can neutralize odors. Wear gloves while using—it's more caustic than baking soda.

WHITE BREAD Bread can absorb oil and moisture. Use a slice to remove smudges from walls, nonwashable wallpaper, wool carpets, and paintings.

WHITE VINEGAR Acidic white vinegar has many household uses. It can be used as a stain remover, a mild bleach, and to add sparkle to glassware and windows.

WORCESTERSHIRE SAUCE A condiment made of water, vinegar, molasses, corn syrup, salt, anchovies, and other spices, Worcestershire sauce can hide scratches in wood furniture and polish tarnished copper pots and brass fixtures.

WAXING and POLISHING

LINSEED OR JOJOBA OIL These natural plant oils may be used to clean wood furniture with an oil finish or unsealed hardwood floors.

POLISH

FURNITURE Your go-to solution for polishing wood furniture and maintaining shine.

METAL There's a variety of commercial metal polishes available for different types of metal (copper, aluminum, silver, and so on).

VODKA Use it to clean your diamonds and other gemstones. Buy at liquor stores.

WAX

CAR Besides making your car shiny, car wax can also help remove grease from wood cabinets and prevent stains on plastic or metal outdoor furniture.

FURNITURE Shines and protects furniture and other finished surfaces such as lacquer, varnish, shellac, polyurethane, or wax finishes. Also ideal for filling in small scuffs and scratches.

STAIN REMOVAL and LAUNDRY

DELICATE WASH A specially formulated laundry soap for fragile fibers, including washable woolens, cashmere, lingerie, nylon, silk, and linen.

DETERGENTS

BABY Harsh detergents can irritate newborns' skin, so baby detergents are made to leave fabric soft and additive-free. Use them for cleaning delicate fabrics too.

LAUNDRY There's a wide variety of detergents from which to choose. Powdered detergents work best if you have hard water; they're great for removing mud and clay. Liquid detergents are good for taking out grease, oily dirt, and stains, and work very well as a pretreatment.

MILD A mild detergent is one that has a neutral or near-neutral pH. Look for detergents that are labeled "gentle for your hands" or "good for hand-washables."

DRY-CLEANING SOLVENT Apply it to stains that are caused by substances that are non-water-soluble, such as butter or grease. Dry-cleaning solvents can be used on clothing or upholstered furniture.

ENZYME-BASED PRESOAKS AND CLEANERS
Enzymes help remove organic and protein-based stains such as blood, perspiration, and pet-related spots.

FABRIC SOFTENER There are three kinds of softeners: liquid (added to the machine during the final rinse); sheets (used in the dryer); and liquid and powder detergents.

TALCUM POWDER Sprinkle it on oily stains to absorb them.

UPHOLSTERY SHAMPOO Ideal for spot-cleaning or to clean upholstery from top to bottom. Make sure the upholstery shampoo you use is safe for your fabric.

ODOR FIXERS

ACTIVATED CHARCOAL This extremely porous substance absorbs and filters odors. Buy at stores that sell aquarium supplies.

CHALK Chalk is a desiccant—it attracts water and can remove excessive humidity that would normally degrade or even destroy products sensitive to moisture.

COFFEE GROUNDS Dried coffee grounds make a great odor absorber.

CORNMEAL This milled grain can be used to absorb stains and non-flammable liquids from fabrics.

ESSENTIAL OILS Eucalyptus, lavender, and other oils can help remove stains, kill bacteria, and add a lovely fragrance to your home. Where to buy: Natural-foods stores, natural health or beauty stores, or reputable online purveyors.

KITTY LITTER Clay-based kitty litter is a great absorbent that will soak up odors as well as oil and grease spills.

ABOUT

Mrs. MEYER'S
CLEAN DAY

by Monica Nassif

When I think of my mother, I think of her gift for finding joy in the everyday. She sighs with happiness at freshly folded towels or watching children make up a game. She points out every blossoming flower; she loves a perfect bowl of oatmeal; she takes true pleasure in a stolen afternoon nap.

Her family and our home were her work. Real work. Joyful work. The way you kept a house going with a big family that "God blessed you with" was by running the house like an athletic team or work crew. We had chores, rules, schedules, crafts, cooking, gardening, mowing—all to feed, clothe, and grow a family. You made do and you made it work. Before recycling, before eco-friendly, there was my mom, who taught us that you can throw out in a teaspoon what you bring home in a bushel. You didn't waste, you didn't squander.

My mother had a large maroon station wagon that she drove like a bat out of hell to grocery stores, football practice, music lessons, and anywhere else the nine of us had to go. As the oldest girl—Mom's second in command—I got to ride up front. I remember asking her once how she knew where she was going. "You learn by just going," she said. That stuck with me.

"I created her and she created me."
—THELMA MEYER ON MONICA NASSIF

I decided to start my own business about ten years ago, while I was standing in a supermarket aisle, eyeing the cleaning products. They were toxic and unattractively packaged. What an insult to the consumer, I thought. There's got to be another way.

When it came time to give the cleaning products a name and a philosophy, I used everything Mom taught me: Find the joy in everything, work hard, and don't waste a thing. That meant using earth-friendly products, never testing on animals, and making the products perfectly safe for use, even around the little ones. It meant bringing a little bit of joy to homemaking through great-looking products that smell garden fresh. Most important, with Mom's name on the label, doing it right meant that the products had to work like the dickens.

Today, we make more than one hundred different hardworking products, from baby detergent to dishwashing soap. You can buy Mrs. Meyer's products at grocery, home, and hardware stores across the country. You can also buy products at **WWW.MRSMEYERS.COM.**

ABOUT the CONTRIBUTORS

THELMA MEYER uses her namesake cleansers around her home in Iowa as well as in her camper in Arizona, where she goes with her husband, Vern, in the winter. She offers advice—both solicited and unsolicited—to her nine children and their spouses, children, and friends.

MONICA NASSIF is the Founder and President of Mrs. Meyer's Clean Day. After serving for more than eighteen years as a brand builder for leading retailer and consumer-product companies, Nassif cofounded a marketing design firm and grew it to one of the largest in the Upper Midwest. She started her marketing career with Target Corporation, a leading U.S. retailer. She lives in Minneapolis with her husband, David, and has two daughters, Calla and Aundrea.

WERNER DESIGN WERKS, INC. (designers) Sharon Werner and Sarah Nelson Forss have garnered national and international awards and honors. WDW's work is included in *100 World's Best Posters* and is part of the permanent collection of the Library of Congress, Musée de la Poste, Victoria and Albert Museum, Musée des Arts Decoratifs, and the Cooper Hewitt Museum. This recognition is not limited to the pages of design annuals; their success has secured them clients such as Moët Hennessey, Target, Mrs. Meyer's Clean Day, Rizzoli, Chronicle Books, and Blu Dot, just to name a few.

NICOLE SFORZA (writer) is a magazine editor who thinks household cleaning wipes are the cat's meow. Her work has appeared in *Wine Spectator*, *Home*, and *Real Simple* magazines, and websites such as Quamut.com. She holds a master's degree in English Education from New York University and currently lives in New York City. She would like to thank her family, including Nicholas, Cara, Mary, and Paul.

ACKNOWLEDGMENTS

Like cleaning the house, making a book requires a lot of elbow grease. Thank you to Nicole Sforza, for the hours of interviews and wonderfully written text. As for the nifty-looking design and inspiring illustrations, thank you to Sharon Werner and Sarah Nelson Forss at Werner Design Werks. Their great style, wit, and wisdom informed every nook and cranny of this book.

Thanks especially to the entire Mrs. Meyer's Clean Day team, particularly Michelle Sahlstrom, who painstakingly checked every word of every draft. Special thanks also to Pamela Helms, the real chemist of the group, who tests Thelma's tricks every day.

Thank you to the team at Melcher Media, including Joel Bernstein, David E. Brown, Daniel Del Valle, Lauren Nathan, Lia Ronnen, Jessi Rymill, Lindsey Stanberry, Alex Tart, Anna Thorngate, Anna Wahrman, Rebecca Wiener, and Betty Wong. The team at Grand Central Publishing, especially Natalie Kaire, Diana Baroni, Jamie Raab, Les Pockell, Deb Futter, and Erica Gelbard, have been excited and incredibly supportive of this book every step of the way.

Finally, thank you to the mothers who taught us to clean up after ourselves, not to waste anything (especially time), and to find work that brings us joy, especially Viola Werner, Helen Nelson, Marllynn Bonn, Dorothy Bonn, Cara Sforza, Mary Sforza, Linda Volkmar, and Joyce Helms.

THANKS MOM.

THIS BOOK WAS PRODUCED BY: Melcher Media   124 West 13th Street, New York, NY 10011   www.melcher.com

PUBLISHER: Charles Melcher
ASSOCIATE PUBLISHER: Bonnie Eldon
EDITOR IN CHIEF: Duncan Book
PRODUCTION DIRECTOR: Kurt Andrews

SENIOR EDITOR and PROJECT MANAGER: Holly Rothman
ASSOCIATE EDITOR: Shoshana Thaler
EDITORIAL ASSISTANT: Coco Joly

INDEX

A

Accessories, 96
Acrylic, 40
 countertops, 54
 furniture, 102
 sinks, 76
Albums, photo, 142–143
Aluminum
 deck, 185
 outdoor furniture, 199
 saucepans, 44
Animals, 104, 170–171,
 196, 202, *202*.
 See also Pests; Pets;
 specific animals
Antique wood, 102
Ants, 222
Appliances. *See also*
 specific appliances
 countertop, 41
 monthly cleaning for, 20
 spring cleaning for, 23
Artwork, 115, 178, *178*
Asphalt, repair of, 206
Attic, 179–180, *180*
Attitude, about cleaning, 11
Avonite. *See* Solid surface

B

Baby, *160*
 clothes, *152*, 160–161
 room, 122
Backsplashes, 42
Baking
 with children, 60, *60*, 61, *61*
 soda, 28, *28*, 156, *156*
Bamboo floors, 90
Banisters, 179
Bank accounts, 141
Baseboards, 177
Basement, 180
 odors in, 221
Bathroom, 62–88
 cabinets, 71
 ceiling heater for, 78
 fan for, 78

for impromptu company,
 26, 68–69
odors in, 66, 78, *78*, 220
overview for, 64–65
safety in, 79–83
on Saturday, 33
toolbox for, 66, *66*
triage in, 80, *80*, 81, *81*
ventilation for, 78
Bedroom, 108–127.
 See also Baby
 children and, 109, 152
 cleaning products for, 112
 cleaning times for, 123, *123*
 floors, 114
 furnishings, 113
 overview for, 110–111
 privacy for, 109, *109*
 storage in, 121
 toolbox for, 112, *112*
 upholstery, 113
Beds, 23, 117, 121, *121*
 making, 118, *118*, 119, *119*
Beer, 101, 169
Birdbaths, 202, *202–203*
Blankets, 155, 183, 184.
 See also Comforters; Quilts
Bleach, safety v., 63
Blender, 41, *41*
Blinds, 93, 115, *115*
Blood, 101, 160, 168
Books, 120, *120*, 135
Bookshelves, 134
Boys (twin), *14*, 16, 161, *161*.
 See also specific boys
Bras, 153, 158, *159*, *212*
Brass, 46
 accessories, 96
 fireplace, 97
Brick driveway, 206
Broom, *10*
Bucket, 185, *185*
Buffing, for floors, 74–75
Bugs, in foods, 223
Burned pot, 43
Butcher block countertops, 55
Butter, 101

Buttons, 183
 sewing on, 187

C

Cabinets, 52
 bathroom, 71
 medicine, 71
Cages, for pets, 217
Can opener, 41
Candlelight, 27, 68–69
Canning, 58–59
Carpets, 20, 91, 114, 157
 formula on, 122
 indentations in, 90
 on kitchen floors, 57
 stain removal for, 105
 vacuuming for, 89
Carrots, story about, 82,
 82, 83, *83*
Cars, *207*, 208
Cashmere, 182
Cast iron saucepans, 44, 45
Cats, *104*, 171, *171*, *214*,
 216–217, *217*
Caulk, 68, 72
Cedar
 blocks of, 184, *184*
 chest, 150
Ceiling, 93, *93*
 fans, 116
Ceramic saucepans, 44
Ceramic tile, 67
 countertops, 54
 floor buffing for, 74
CFLs. *See* Compact
 fluorescent lightbulbs
Chairs, 84–85, 100–101, *108*
Charcoal grill, 197
Charging, cordless phone, 138
Chenille, 100
Children. *See also* Baby;
 Kids; *specific children*
 baking with, 60, *60*, 61, *61*
 bedrooms and, 109, 152
 chores for, 39, 116
 cleaning by, 12–13
 computer's control v., 137

sewing and, 186, 188,
 188, 189, *189*
 stain remover and, 152, *152*
Chocolate, *126*, 126–127
 stain removal for, 101, 168
Cigarette odors, 221, *221*
Cleaning. *See also* Pets;
 specific household items
 attitude about, 11
 by children, 12–13
 while cooking, 35
 daily/weekly/monthly, 20,
 123
 fall, 24–25
 neighbors and, 212–213
 organization in, 11–12
 prevention v., 36
 sleeping and, 125
 spring, 23
 windows, *21*, 22, *23*, 24, 42
 yearly, 21, 123
Cleaning supply(ies), 30–31.
 See also Toolbox
 baking soda as, 28, *28*,
 156, *156*
 for bathroom, 66
 for bedrooms, 112
 brushes as, 29
 in cleaning supply list, 29
 for kitchen, 38
 lemon juice as, 28
 for living room, 88
 for nooks and crannies, 176
 safety and, 13, 28, 185
 toothpaste as, 77
 in utility closet, 185
 vinegar as, 28
Closets, 21, 121, 181, *181*,
 183, 185
Clothes, 145.
 See also Ironing; Laundry;
 specific types of clothes
 baby, *152*, 160–161
 donation of, 181
 laundry labels for, 166,
 166, 167, *167*
 mothproofing for, 184
 stain removal for, 166,
 166, 167, *167*, 168–169
 storage of, 150, 182, *182*
Cobwebs, 196

Coffee
  for gardens, 200
  stain, on clothes, 169
Coffeemaker, 41, *41*
Coir rugs, 91
Cola, for rust stains, 71
Comforters, 155, 183
Compact fluorescent
  lightbulbs (CFLs), 95
Composite deck, 185
Compost, how to, 204–205
Computers, 133–134
  children v., 137
  recycling for, 139
Concrete, 206
Consumption, of water, 13
Cooking, 60–61
  cleaning while, 35
Copper, 40, 44, 46
Cords, 136
  phone, 138
Corduroy, 100
Corian. *See* Solid surface
Cotton, 100
  button-down shirts, 151, 164
  dresses, 153
Countertop appliances, 41
Countertops, 54
Coupons, 50
Crabgrass, 203
Cradle, rocking, 122, *122*
Crawl space, 173
  dehumidifying, 180
Crayon
  on clothes, 168
  on upholstery, 114
  on walls, 92
Cucumbers, 201
Curtains, 157.
  See also Drapes
Cushions, outdoor, 198
Cutting boards, 55, *55*

D

Daily cleaning
  aspects of, 20
  bedroom, 123
Days, for specific tasks, 32–33
Decals, for tub, 72

Deck, 185, 191
Decoration, unexpected,
  106–107
Dehumidifying, 180
Denture tablets, for toilet, 71
Desks, 134
Diapers, 160
Dishwasher, 49
Disinfecting. *See also*
  Bathroom; Kitchen
  for phone, 138
Dogs, *104, 214*, 216–217, *217*
Dolls, 98, 109
Doorknobs, 96
Drainpipes, 211
Drains, 39, 72, *72*
Drapes, 92, 114
  cord safety and, 115
Dresser drawers, 113
Dresses
  cotton, 153
  wedding/formal, 182
Driveway, 206
Dry-clean, hand wash v., 154
Dryer
  cleaning for, 165
  hang dry v., 149
  vent, 165
Dusting, 20
  paintbrush for, 178

E

Electric fireplace, 97
Electronics, 98, 135
  recycling for, 139
Enameled cast iron
  saucepans, 45
Entertainment, 98–99
Entryways, 177

F

Fabric, 100–101.
  See also specific fabrics
  shades, 93
  softener, 156
Fall cleaning, 24–25
Fan, for bathroom, 78
Farmer's Almanac, 201
Faucets, kitchen sink, 39

Federal Trade Commission
  (ftc.gov), about junk mail,
  136
Fertilization, for grass, 195
Fiberglass walls, 67
Fingerprints, on banisters, 179
Fireplace, 97
  artwork v., 178
  fall cleaning for, 24
  when to clean, 21
First aid kit, 80, *80*, 81, *81*
First impressions, 26
Fleas, pets and, 216
Fleece pullovers, 153
Flies, 223
Flip-flops, 154
Floors, 57, 90, 208
  See also Wood floors
  bedroom, 114
  buffing for, 74–75
  carpet vacuuming for, 89
  mopping for, 73
  safety and, 79
  vacuuming, *23, 25*, 89
Floppy disks, recycling for, 139
Folder, accordion, 140
Formula, 122
  stain removal for, 160
Freezer, defrosting, 50–51
Friday, 33, *33*
Fruit juice, red, 168
Fur coats, 182
Furnace, 24
Furniture
  bedroom, 113
  nonupholstered, 102–103
  outdoor, *23, 25*, 198–199
  pet hair/stains and, 104
  pets v., 219
  spring cleaning for, 22
  upholstered, 100–101
  wood, 102–103, *103*, 199

G

Garage, 207
  stain removal in, 208
Garbage cans, 51, *220*
  monthly cleaning for, 20
Garbage disposal, 51

Gardens, 190–191
  care for, 200
  fall cleaning in, 25
  vegetables in, 201
Gas fireplace, 97
Gas grill, 197
Gift-wrapping area, 179, *179*
Giraffe, decorative, *106,*
  106–107
Glass.
  See also Mirrors; Window(s)
  cleaning broken, 69, *69*
  over paintings/photographs,
  178
  recycled, floor buffing for, 75
  saucepans, 45
  shower doors, 67
Glass-ceramic saucepans, 44
Gloves, 153–154
Gold, 46
  jewelry, 124
Granite sinks, 76
Grass, 195
  crabgrass v., 203
  stains, 168
Gravel, 206
Grease stains
  in clothes, 168
  on walls, 42
Griddles, 44–45
Grill, 197, *197*
Grout, in shower, 68–69
Gum
  on carpet, 105
  on clothes, 169
Gutters/downspouts, 25, 211

H

Hairspray, on mirrors, 69
Hallways, 177
Hammock, 198
Hamster, *170,* 171
Hands, odors on, 221, *221*
Hang dry, *23, 149*
  kids' help for, 155
  machine v., 149
Hardwood (sealed/unsealed)
  floors, 57, 114
Hats, 153
Heater, for bathroom's
  ceiling, 78

Hemp rugs, 91
Home office, 32, 128–143
 decoration for, 134
 organization in, 135
 overview for, 130–131
 storage in, *128*, 135, *135*
 toolbox for, 132, *132*
Hospital corners, for beds,
 118, *118*
House, outside, 23, 25.
 See also Garage;
 Gardens; Outdoors
Houseplants, 96

I

Ice, cars and, 208
Impromptu company
 bathroom beautification
  for, 26, 68–69
 candlelight for, 27, 68–69
 first impressions for, 26
 kitchen's clean-up for, 27
 scent for, 27
 shimmer/shine for, 26
 triage for, 26–27
Ink, 101, 169
Ink-jet cartridges, recycling
 for, 139
Iron, cleaning of, *162–163*, 165
Iron outdoor furniture, 199
Ironing, *164*
 button-down shirts, 164
 heat for, 164
 how-to, 162–163
 pants, 164
 silk ties, 164
 tablecloths, 164
 on Tuesday, 32

J

Jackets, down-filled, 153
JC Penny catalog, 98
Jeans, 151
 storage for, 182
Jewelry, 124, *124*
Juice/soft drinks, 101
Junk mail, 136
Jute rugs, 91

K

Ketchup, 40
Keyboard, computer, 133
Kids, 52. *See also*
 My House, My Rules
 choosing outfits for, 121
 eating locations for, 91
 exercise/competition for,
  196
 hang drying with, 155
 reading for, 120
 traveling with, 207
Kitchen, 34–61
 cleaning supplies for, 38
 as command central, 34
 details in, 36–37
 floors, 57
 for impromptu company, 27
 odors in, 220
 overview for, 36–37
 on Saturday, 33
 sink, 39–40
 toolbox for, 38
Knickknacks, 96, 120
 fixing, 127
Knives, 47, *47*
Knobs
 door, 96
 oven, 43

L

Labels
 on furniture, 100
 for laundering clothes,
  166, *166*, 167, *167*
Lacquer, 102
Ladder, *210*, 211
Laminate
 cabinets, 53
 countertops, 54
 floor buffing for, 74
 kitchen floors, 57
Lamp shades, *94*, 95
Laptop computer, 134
Laundry, *21, 144, 145,*
 145–165, *165*, 166–171.
 See also Ironing; Stain
 removal
 cleaning supply list for, 30
 clothes labels for, 166,
  166, 167, *167*
 dry-clean v. hand wash, 154
 for Monday, 32

for odor, 144, 165
 overview for, 146–147
 soap for, 150
 sorting of, 149
 time v., 144
 toolbox for, 148, *148*
Laundry room
 maintenance of, 165
 organization of, 145
Lavender, 184, *184*
Lawn mower, 25
Leaks
 fall cleaning for, 24
 weather stripping for, 24
Leather, 100, 154
 bags, 182
 coats, 182
Leftovers, 48
Lemon juice, 28, *28*
Lights, 94, *94*, 95, *95*
 bedroom, 113
 outdoor, 196
Limestone sinks, 76
Linen, 100
 closet, 183, *183*
Lingerie. *See also*
 Bras; Pantyhose;
 Underwear
 discretion for, 159
Linoleum
 countertops, 54
 floor buffing for, 74
 kitchen floors, 57
Lint trap, dryer, 165
Litter box, 217
Living room, 84–107
 activities in, 84–85
 on Friday, 33
 overview for, 86–87
 toolbox for, 88, *88*
Low-flow showerhead, 68

M

Makeup
 safety for, 71
 stain removal for, 169
Marble
 countertops, 54
 sinks, 76
Marigolds, 201
Mascara, 169

Mattress
 pads, 156
 stain removal for, 117
Medicine cabinet, 71
Memories. *See also*
 My House, My Rules;
  specific family members
 albums/scrapbooks for,
  142, 142–143, *143*
 of dining outside, 202
 of exercise/competition, 196
 of holiday's dishwashing, 48
 of hotel soap, 208
 photo albums for, 142–143
 of quick showers, 67
 of sewing, 186
 of summer dinners, 200
 of unexpected decoration,
  106–107
 of water recycling, 151
Mending, 32. *See also*
 Sewing
Metal blinds, 93
Meyer, Daniel Dennis (Dan),
 15, 18, *18*, 48, *48*, 107,
 209
Meyer, Jane Cecelia, *15*, 17,
 17, 151, *151*, 188–189,
 200, *200*, 209
Meyer, Joseph Paul, *15*, 18,
 18, 83, 202, *202*
Meyer, Maria Joan, *15*, 17,
 17, 60–61, 116, *116*,
 126–127, 171, 209
Meyer, Monica Rose, *14*,
 16, *16*, 60–61, 98, 173
Meyer, Patrick John (Pat),
 15, 18, *18*, 67, *67*, 82–83
Meyer, Teresa Ann, *15, 17,*
 17, 171, 173, 186, *186*,
 188–189
Meyer, Thelma A., 9.
 See also My House,
 My Rules
 on cleaning, 11–13
 family of, *14*, 15–18, *19*
Meyer, Thomas Henry (Tom),
 14, 16, *16*, 196, *196*,
 212–213
Meyer, Timothy Joseph (Tim),
 14, 16, *16*, 208, *208*,
 212–213
Meyer, Vernis Henry (Vern),
 10, *14*, 106–107, 128–129,
 172, 191, 209

Mice, 223

Microwave, 48

Mildew, from caulk, 68

Milk, 160, 169

Mineral stains, in sinks, 76

Mirrors, 69, 69

Mixer, 41, *41*

Mold, artwork v., 178

Monday, 32, *32*

Monitor, computer, 133

Monthly cleaning, 20

Mopping, 73, *73*

Mops, *10*, 75, *75*

Mothproofing, 184

Motor home, 209, *209*

Mouse, computer, 134

Mowing, for grass, 195

Mudrooms, 177, *177*

Mulch, 200

My House, My Rules
  appearance for pride,
    149, *149*
  closets, 181, *181*
  coupons for, 50, *50*
  dinner bell for, 51, *51*
  gift-wrapping area, 179, *179*
  home office decoration,
    134, *134*
  important papers, 133,
    133
  on kids' eating, 91, *91*
  of kids' hang drying, 155,
    155
  on kids' outfits, 121, *121*
  on kids' reading, 120, *120*
  knickknacks, 96, *96*
  phone calls, 138, *138*
  on rocking cradle, 122, *122*
  shining wood floors, 89, *89*
  special quilts, 156, *156*
  towels' size, 157, *157*
  traveling with kids, 207,
    207

N

Nail polish, for threads, 186

Napkins, table, 157

Neighbors, *212*, 212–213,
  213

Nonstick saucepans, 45

Nook, for sewing, 172–173

Nooks and Crannies, *172*,
  172–189
  artwork for, 178
  overview for, 174–175
  toolbox for, 176, *176*

Nylon stockings, for tub, 72

O

Odors
  in basement, 221
  in bathroom, 66, 78, *78*,
    220
  cigarette, 221
  cleaning supply list for, 31
  from dishwasher, 49
  from garbage disposal, 51
  on hands, 221
  impromptu company and,
    27
  in kitchen, 220
  laundry for, 144, 165
  pets and, 216–218
  from produce, 52
  refrigerator, 50, 221, *221*
  from sneakers, 220

Onions, 201

Organization
  of attic, 180
  of basement, 180
  in cleaning, 11–12
  for closets, 181
  of cords, 136
  of garage, 207
  in home office, 135
  of laundry room, 145
  for mudroom/entryway, 177

Ottomans, 100–101

Outdoor furniture
  cleaning for, *198*, 198–199
  fall cleaning and, 25
  spring cleaning for, 23

Outdoors, 190–208
  cleaning supply list for, 31
  overview for, 192–193
  toolbox for, 194, *194*

Outside painting, 25, *25, 213*

Oven
  cleaning, 21
  interior, 43
  knobs, 43
  stove top, 43
  vent hood, 43

P

Painted wood, 102
  windows, 105

Painting, outside, 25, *25*, 213

Pants
  dress, 151
  ironing, 164
  sewing of, 187
  sweatpants, 153

Pantyhose, 158

Papers, 141
  management of, 140, *140*

Paper-shredder, 136

Parsley, 201

Patio furniture, 198, *198*

Pearl jewelry, 124

Pellet fireplace, 97

Peppers, 201

Perspiration, on clothes, 169

Pesticide, natural, 201, 202

Pests, *214, 222, 223*
  prevention and, 222–223

Pets, 104, 170–171
  cleaning for, *214*, 216–219
  furniture v., 219
  odors and, 216–218
  safety for, 219
  skunks and, 218

Pewter, 46

Phone, *138*
  cell, recycling for, 139
  cordless, charging of, 138

Photographs, 142–143

Piano, 98

Pictures, *96*, 115
  frames, 96, 115, 178

Pillowcases, 155

Pillows, 117, 155

Place mats, 52

Plants, 96, *190*.
  See also Grass
  cats and, 216
  hanging, 196
  potted, 197

Plastic. *See also* Vinyl
  bags, 49, 205
  clothes storage v., 150, 182
  outdoor furniture, 199

Porcelain, 40
  sinks, 76

Porch, 196–197

Pots, 43, *49*

Pressure cooker, 58–59

Prevention. *See also* Safety
  cleaning v., 36
  pests and, 222–223

Printer, computer, 134

Privacy
  motor home vacations
    and, 209
  for parents, 109

Q

Quilts, 156. *See also*
  Comforters

R

Radishes, 201

Recliners, *84*, 84–85

Recycled glass, floor buffing
  for, 75

Recycling. *See also*
  Waste Not Want Not
  for electronics, 139
  in garage, 207
  of water, 151, 197

Refrigerator, 51
  odors in, 50, 221, *221*

Renyer, Cleta, 42

Rest, Sunday for, 33

Rhubarb, 201

Roaches, 222

Rugs, 167
  cleaning for, 91

Rust stains
  in clothes, 168
  in toilet, 71

S

Safe deposit box, 140

Safety
  in bathrooms, 79–83
  bleach v., 63
  for canning, 58–59
  cleaning products and,
    13, 28, 185
  for cutting boards, 55
  drape cords and, 115
  fall cleaning for, 24
  floors and, 79
  for grass mowing, 195
  for makeup, 71

for medicine, 71
for pets, 219
spring cleaning for, 22
Samsung Staron.
See Solid surface
Saturday, 33, *33*
Saucepans, 44–45
Save your energy, 12–13
Scarves, 153
Scrapbooks, *142*, 142–143, *143*
Scratching post, 216, *216*
Screens
cathode-ray tube, 133
porch, 196
Scuff marks, on wood floors, 90
Sewing
buttons, 187
children and, 186, 188, *188*, 189, *189*
kit, 186, *186*
nook for, 172–173
tips for, 187
Shades, fabric, 93
Sheets, 155
storage of, 183
Shirts, cotton button-down, 151
ironing, 164
Shoes, in house, 56, *56*
Shopping, 33
Shower, 67
caulk in, 68
curtains, 68, 156
grout in, 68–69
showerhead in, 68
tracks/frames/rods, 68
Silicone saucepans, 45
Silk, 100
storage for, 182
ties, ironing for, 164
Silver, 46
jewelry, 124
Silverware, 46, *46*
Sinks, *21, 39,* 39–40, 76, *77*
Sisal rugs, 91
Skunks, 218, *218*
Sleeping, trouble with, 125
Slippers, 154

Slugs, in gardens, 200
Smoke detectors, 22
Sneakers, 154, *154, 220*
odors from, 220
Soap, *34*
chips, 78
from hotels, 208
laundry, 150
Socks, 153, *154*
Sofas, 100–101
Solid surface
countertops, 55
sinks, 40, 76
Soy sauce, 169
Speakers, 98
Spiders, 223
Spring cleaning, 22–23
Squeegee, 67
Stain removal, 42, 88, 166–167
for baby clothes, 160
from carpets, 105
cat urine, 217
for children's bedrooms, 152, *152*
cleaning supply list for, 30
food stains, 101, 160, 168–169
on garage floor, 208
for makeup, 169
for mattresses, 117
of milk, 160, 169
promptness for, 165
upholstered furniture, 100–101
Stainless steel, 46
cabinets, 53
countertops, 55
kitchen sink, 40
saucepans, 45
Stairs, 179, *221*
Staples (store), for recycling, 139
Statue, story about, *126*, 126–127, *127*
Steel outdoor furniture, 199
Sterilizing jars, 58–59
Stone
driveway of, 206
floor buffing for, 75
kitchen sink, 40
limestone sinks, 76

Storage
in bedrooms, 121, *121*
of clothes, 150, 182, *182*
in home office, *128*, 135, *135*
of patio furniture, 198
of table linens, 183
Stove top, 43
Suits, 182
Sunday, 33, *33*
Sunlight, artwork v., 178
Sunroom, 191
Sweaters, 150
Sweatpants/shirts, 153
Swimsuits, 158
Switch plates, 115
SYE. See Save your energy
Synthetic rugs, 91

T

Table, 52
Table linens, 157, *157*
ironing, 164
storage, 183
Teak outdoor furniture, 199
Telephone. See Phone
Television, 98–99, *99*
Thermofoil cabinets, 53
Thriftiness, 68, 208. *See also* Waste Not Want Not
Thursday, 33, *33*
Tile
acoustic, 93
ceramic (glazed/unglazed), 54, 67, 74
Time, laundry v., 144
Toaster, 41
Toilets, 21, *62*, 71, *220*
brush for, *70*
Tomatoes, 201
Toolbox (cleaning supplies)
for bathroom, 66, *66*
for bedrooms, 112, *112*
for home office, 132, *132*
for kitchen, 38, *38*
for laundry, 148, *148*
for living room, 88, *88*
for nooks and crannies, 176, *176*
for outdoors, 194, *194*

Toothpaste
for cleaning, 77
on mirrors, 69
Tossing
old foods, 52
spring cleaning for, 23
Towels, 157, *157*, 183
Tower, computer, 133
Trash bags, decomposition of, 205
Triage
bathroom, 80, *80*, 81, *81*
for impromptu company, 26–27
T-Shirts, 153
Tub, 72
mat, 79
Tuesday, 32, *32*
Typewriter, 137, *137*

U

Umbrella, outdoor, 198
Underwear, 153, 158
Upholstery. *See also specific upholstered furniture*
bedroom, 113
crayon from, 114
Utility closets, 185

V

Vacuuming
beds, 117
floors, *23, 25,* 89
stairs, 179
Vegetables, in gardens, 201
Velvet, 100
Venetian blinds, 115, *115*
Vent hood (stove), 43
Ventilation
for attic, 179
for bathroom, 78
Vents
dryer, 165
heating, 114
when to clean, 21
Vinegar, 28, *28*
Vinyl
blinds, 93
floor buffing for, 75
kitchen floors, 57

W

Wallpaper, 115

Walls, 92, 114–115
  fiberglass, 67
  fingerprints on, 177
  grease stains on, 42

Washcloths, 42

Washing machine, 165

Waste Not Want Not.
  See also Recycling
  absorb moisture, 135
  buttons, 183
  ceiling fans v. air
    conditioner, 117
  CFLs for, 95
  condiments and, 51
  dishcloths for, 42
  dry-clean v. hand wash, 154
  fabric softener, 156
  iron heat, 164
  kids' dinners, 52
  laundry soap, 150
  leftovers for, 48
  low-flow showerhead for, 68
  plastic bags for, 49
  prompt stain removal, 165
  soap chips, 78
  used dryer sheets, 133

Water
  for compost, 204
  consumption of, 13
  for grass, 195
  recycling of, 151, 197
  rings, 105
  softener for, 67

Waxing/polishing, 30
  floor buffing as, 74–75

Weather stripping, 24

Websites
  for junk mail, 136
  for recycling electronics, 139

Wedding/formal dresses, 182

Wednesday, 32, *32*

Weekly cleaning, 20, 123

Welcome mats, 177

White bread, for cleaning, 177

Wicker, 102
  outdoor furniture, 199

Window(s)
  cleaning, *21, 22, 23,* 24,
    42, *42*
  fall cleaning for, 24
  painted-shut, 105

  spring cleaning for, 22
  windshield as, 208

Wine, 101
  on clothes, 169

Wipers, 29

Wood
  antique, 102
  blinds, 93
  -burning fireplace, 97
  cabinets, 53, 71
  furniture, 102–103, *103,*
    113
  outdoor furniture, 199
  painted, 102, 105
  treated, as deck, 185
  water rings from, 105

Wood floors
  care for, 89
  hardwood, 57, 114
  scuff marks, 90
  sealed/unsealed, 90
  waxing, 90

Wool, 100
  rugs, 91
  sweaters' storage, 182

Workout wear, 153

Y

Yearly cleaning, 21
  bedroom, 123

a **CLEAN HOME** is a **HAPPY HOME**